GCSE English

An Inspector Calls

by J.B. Priestley

If you're studying *An Inspector Calls*, this superb CGP Text Guide has everything you need to score the best possible grades for your GCSE exams.

We've explained the whole play — characters, language, themes, historical background... it's all in here. And because it's a CGP book, everything's written in a chatty style that's easy to understand.

But that's not all. We've also included plenty of practice questions, and there's a whole section of advice on how to plan and structure answers that'll dazzle the examiners!

The Text Guide

CONTENTS

CONTENTS

Published by CGP

Editors:
Claire Boulter
Holly Corfield-Carr
Emma Crighton
Luke von Kotze
Anthony Muller
Rachael Powers

Contributor:
Peter Needham

With thanks to Jennifer Underwood and Paula Barnett for the proofreading.

With thanks to:

Cover photograph by Owen Howells with kind permission of The Torch Theatre, Milford Haven

Photos of An Inspector Calls at Lamb's Players Theatre, Coronado, California / directed by Robert Smyth / cast: Glynn Bedington, Jilian Frost, David Cochran Heath, Jon Lorenz, Colleen Kollar Smith. Lance Arthur Smith, Robert Smyth / photos by Ken Jacques and Nathan Peirson

With thanks to Simon Gough Photography for permission to use the images on pages 3, 5, 6, 9, 10, 11, 12, 13, 22, 24, 25, 26, 28, 31, 41, 42, 43 & 48

With thanks to Chesil Theatre Winchester for permission to use the images on pages 3 & 27

With thanks to Rex Features for permission to use the images on pages 3, 4, 11, 12, 19, 20, 21, 26, 48 & 49

Images on pages 8, 23 & 24 © WATERGATE PRODS / THE KOBAL COLLECTION

With thanks to Mary Evans Picture Library for permission to use the images on pages 1, 2, 29 & 36

With thanks to iStockphoto.com for permission to use the images on pages 3 & 32

With thanks to TopFoto.co.uk for permission to use the images on pages 3, 5 & 50

With thanks to Getty Images for permission to use the images on pages 1 & 39

Image on page 33: Women working in a factory (b/w photo) by English Photographer, (20th century) National Army Museum, London/ The Bridgeman Art Library

ISBN: 978 1 84146 115 1

Printed by Elanders Ltd, Newcastle upon Tyne.

Clipart from Corel®

Introducing 'An Inspector Calls' and J.B. Priestley

An Inspector Calls is about society and class divides

- J.B. Priestley <u>wrote</u> *An Inspector Calls* in <u>1945</u>, during the Second World War, but he <u>set</u> the play in <u>1912</u>.

- In 1912, society wasn't <u>equal</u> — <u>people</u> with more <u>money</u> and from a <u>higher</u> class had more power.

- Priestley used the unequal society of <u>1912</u> as a setting to get people to think about <u>inequality</u> in <u>1945</u>.

An Inspector Calls has a strong message...

1) The audience knows that the characters' world is going to go through terrible changes. 1912 was just before the <u>First World War</u> — which began in 1914 and killed millions of people.

2) Priestley wrote *An Inspector Calls* to <u>challenge</u> his <u>audience</u> to think about how many more <u>disasters</u> lay ahead for them if they didn't learn from <u>past mistakes</u>.

© Mary Evans / Robert Hunt Collection

A wounded soldier receives first aid in a trench during the Battle of the Somme, 1916.

The war years affected J.B. Priestley's life and writing

- *An Inspector Calls* was written near the end of the <u>Second World War</u>, so the audience would have seen how war <u>affected</u> everyone. Soldiers were returning from the war and <u>hoping</u> for a <u>better life</u>.

- *An Inspector Calls* asks the audience to <u>unite</u> to improve <u>society</u>.

1894	Born in <u>Bradford</u>
1910	Left school and started work as a <u>clerk</u> at a wool firm.
1914-18	First World War. Priestley was <u>wounded</u> but survived.
1919-21	Studied for degree in modern history and politics at <u>Cambridge University</u>.
1922	Started work as a <u>journalist</u> in London.
1939	Second World War starts.
1940	Priestley presented a popular BBC <u>radio programme</u>, 'Postscripts', but his show was cancelled after members of the government decided Priestley's views were <u>too</u> <u>left-wing</u> (i.e. socialist).
1941-42	Priestley founded various <u>socialist organisations</u>.
1945	Second World War ends.
1984	Died, aged 89.

© Universal Images Group/Contributor/Hulton Archive /Getty Images

J. B. Priestley

For more about <u>socialism</u>, see p.36.

Background Information

The play's set in Brumley — a fictional town in the Midlands

Brumley is described as an <u>industrial</u> city in the <u>North Midlands</u>. In 1912, cities like this would have had <u>factories</u> and thousands of terraced houses for all the <u>factory workers</u>. Here are the <u>key locations</u> in the play:

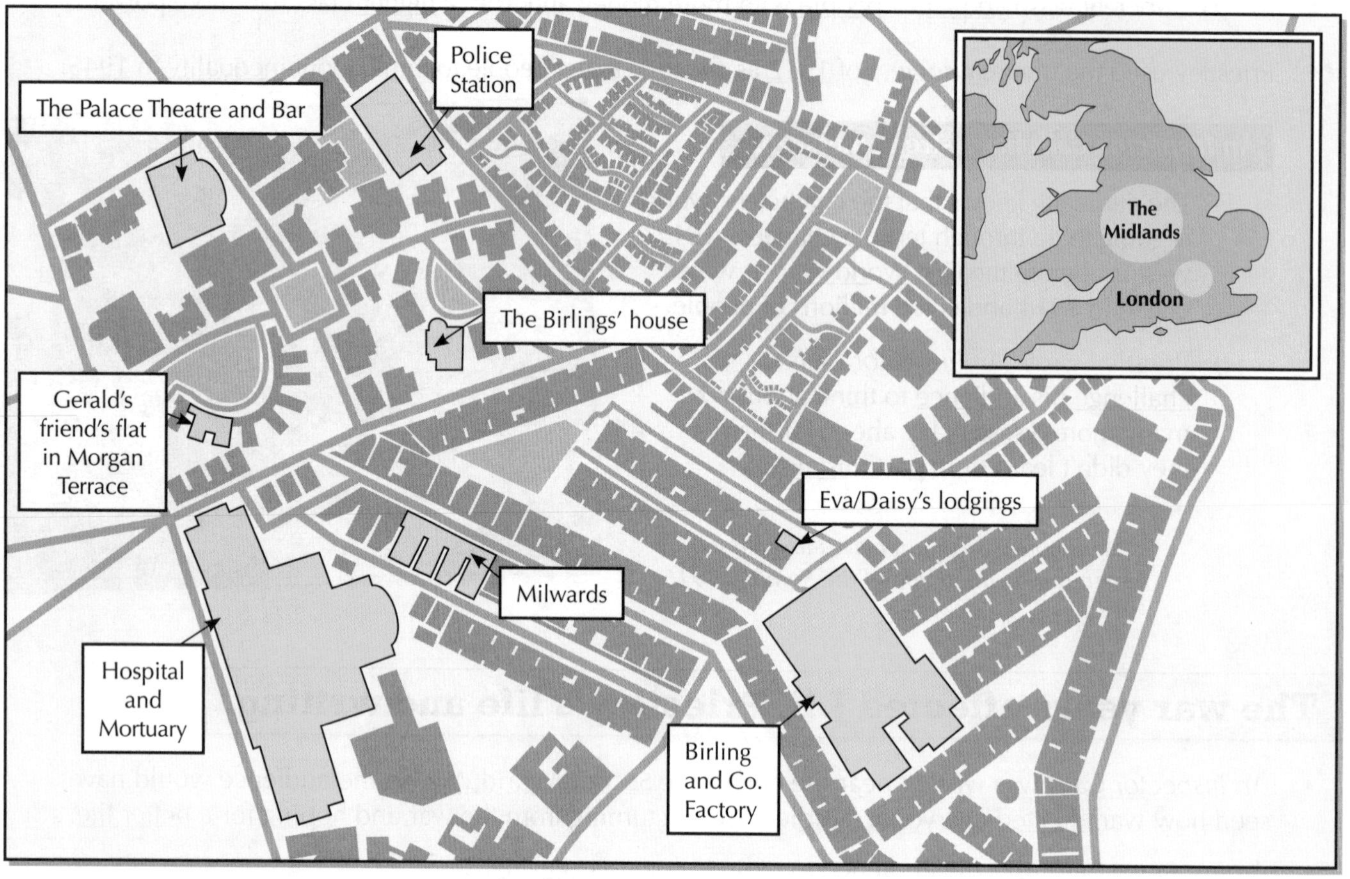

The Palace Theatre and Bar

Police Station

The Birlings' house

Gerald's friend's flat in Morgan Terrace

Eva/Daisy's lodgings

Milwards

Hospital and Mortuary

Birling and Co. Factory

The Midlands

London

Status and wealth kept the classes apart

© Mary Evans Picture Library

Women working in a carpet factory, 1902.

- In 1912 the <u>upper</u> and <u>middle classes</u> lived pretty <u>comfortably</u>. Many middle-class men were wealthy and powerful because they had <u>businesses</u> or <u>professional</u> jobs, e.g. doctors.

- The <u>working classes</u> had a very different life. They had to <u>work hard</u> for <u>little money</u>, often in <u>factories</u> owned by the middle classes.

- People were expected to <u>provide</u> for <u>themselves</u>, so <u>support</u> for those in need was <u>limited</u>.

- This made it <u>difficult</u> for working-class people to <u>help themselves</u> if they fell on <u>hard times</u>.

Introduction

Who's Who in Brumley

Arthur Birling...

... is a successful businessman who is well respected in Brumley. He owns a factory and is head of the Birling family.

Sybil Birling...

... is Arthur's wife. She's obsessed with etiquette and her status in society.

Eric Birling...

... is the Birlings' son. He's a secret alcoholic who's going to inherit his father's business.

Gerald Croft...

... is an upper-class businessman. He's about thirty, and is engaged to Sheila.

Sheila Birling...

... is the Birlings' daughter. She's in her early twenties, and is engaged to Gerald.

The Inspector...

... is a mysterious man who claims to be a police inspector. He's investigating the death of Eva Smith.

Edna...

... is the Birlings' parlour maid. She doesn't have many lines, but she welcomes the Inspector into the house. She's the only working-class woman on stage.

Eva Smith/Daisy Renton...

... is the victim of the play. We never see her. She might be lots of different girls. She might not even be dead...

Introduction

'An Inspector Calls' — Plot Summary

'An Inspector Calls'... what happens when?

Here's a little recap of the <u>main events</u> of *An Inspector Calls*. It's a good idea to learn <u>what happens when</u>, so that you know exactly how the plot progresses and how all the important events fit together.

Act One — one spring evening in 1912...

- The <u>Birling family</u> are celebrating Sheila's <u>engagement</u> to Gerald. It all seems to be going well, but Sheila <u>suspects</u> that Gerald lost interest in her last summer.

- Arthur gives a speech to Eric and Gerald about <u>business</u>. He says that every man should <u>look after himself</u>.

- Inspector Goole arrives and says that a <u>woman</u> called <u>Eva Smith</u> has <u>committed</u> <u>suicide</u> by drinking disinfectant. He starts to question the family members, one by one.

- It turns out Arthur Birling <u>sacked</u> Eva Smith from his factory for <u>striking</u> in <u>protest</u> against <u>low</u> <u>wages</u> and that Sheila asked for Eva Smith to be <u>sacked</u> from a department store last year.

- The Inspector explains that <u>Eva Smith</u> then <u>changed</u> her name to <u>Daisy Renton</u>. Gerald appears shocked and Eric leaves.

Act Two — everyone's tangled up in the Inspector's investigation

- Although he wants to keep it a secret, Gerald eventually describes how he spent last summer with Daisy Renton — she was his <u>mistress</u>.

- Gerald is upset. Sheila <u>returns</u> his ring and Gerald leaves.

- The Inspector gets Sybil to confess that she <u>persuaded</u> the <u>Women's Charity</u> <u>Organisation</u> to <u>reject</u> Eva/Daisy's appeal for help. Eva/Daisy was <u>pregnant</u> at the time.

- Sybil <u>blames</u> the <u>father</u> of Eva/Daisy's child for her death.

- Sheila guesses that the father of the child is <u>Eric</u>.

Act Three — Eric brings shame to the family

- Eric returns. He knows that the Inspector has led everyone to the <u>conclusion</u> that he's the <u>father</u> of Eva/Daisy's <u>unborn child</u>.

- He describes how he met Eva Smith at a bar, and drunkenly <u>forced</u> her to have <u>sex</u>. He got her pregnant and then <u>stole money</u> from his father's office to <u>support</u> her.

- Eva/Daisy <u>rejected</u> the <u>stolen money</u> and turned to Sybil's charity for help. Eric says Sybil <u>murdered</u> her own grandchild by refusing to give her <u>charity</u>.

© Simon Gough Photography

- The Inspector reminds the Birlings that we are all <u>responsible</u> for each other. He warns that unless everyone <u>learns</u> to look after each other, the <u>lesson</u> will have to be learnt later with <u>greater suffering</u>.

Act Three — the final twist...

- Gerald returns, having spoken to a police officer who <u>doesn't recognise</u> the name 'Goole'. Birling calls the police station to confirm there is <u>no inspector</u> called 'Goole' in the area.

© Francis Loney/Arena PAL. TopFoto.co.uk

- Gerald calls the hospital and finds out that no one has <u>committed suicide</u>. Birling, Sybil and Gerald decide it's all been a <u>hoax</u> and start to <u>relax</u>.

- Sheila and Eric argue that they are all still <u>guilty</u> of treating someone badly.

- The phone <u>rings</u>. A young woman has just been found <u>dead</u> after drinking disinfectant, and the police are sending an inspector to <u>question</u> the Birling family...

Ring, ring — this is your future self calling...

...to say thanks for starting off your revision so well. Once you're confident you know <u>what happens when</u> in *An Inspector Calls*, turn over the page to start <u>Section One</u> for some cracking <u>analysis</u> of the <u>plot</u>. If you're still not 100% clear on the plot, turn to the back of the book for the cartoon...

Photo: An Inspector Calls, ©2010 Lamb's Players Theatre

Introduction

Analysis of Act One — Arthur's Speech

After getting to know Priestley and pinning down the plot, it's about time to work out what's really going on. This section will analyse the play, act by act, pointing out key plot points and explaining the play's themes.

The Birlings are having an engagement party

1) Everyone is <u>content</u> and saying the <u>right things</u>.

2) The Birlings are Priestley's <u>idea</u> of a 'perfect' <u>middle-class</u> family:

© Simon Gough Photography

- the father's a successful <u>businessman</u>

- the mother works hard to keep up the Birlings' <u>reputation</u> in the community

- the son <u>works</u> for the father in the <u>family business</u>

- the daughter's <u>engaged</u> to the son of their <u>competitor</u> — this should <u>improve the business</u> because the two companies could <u>merge</u> in the future

But there are hints of conflict under the surface

1) Gerald's family, the Crofts, are <u>more established</u> and <u>socially superior</u>. This makes Arthur Birling anxious.

2) Gerald says he was <u>busy</u> with work last summer. But Sheila's <u>not really satisfied</u> with this answer — "Yes, that's what *you* say."

3) There are <u>big differences</u> between what's expected of <u>men</u> and <u>women</u>. In this society, men are supposed to be busy with <u>work</u> and the world of <u>public affairs</u>. Women are supposed to be interested in <u>family</u>, <u>clothes</u> and <u>social etiquette</u> ('proper' behaviour).

Birling lectures the young men about war and business

KEY EVENT

1) Arthur Birling's <u>confident</u> about the future for his family and business. He gives a <u>speech</u> with his <u>predictions</u> for the <u>future</u>. But the audience of <u>1946</u> knows what's coming, and it's not what Birling thinks:

- He says <u>conflicts</u> between workers and bosses will come to <u>nothing</u>. But there were many strikes between 1912 and 1945, including the <u>General Strike</u> of 1926, which saw the country grind to a halt for nine days.

- He says technological progress will continue, and gives the recently completed Titanic as an example. He says it's "<u>unsinkable</u>, <u>absolutely unsinkable</u>".

- Eric asks whether there'll be a <u>war</u> with Germany. Arthur says <u>no way</u>. But two years later, along comes <u>World War One</u> — war with Germany.

2) Priestley uses dramatic irony to make Birling look <u>overconfident</u>. It makes the audience think that Birling might be wrong about lots of other things, such as his belief in the motto '<u>Every man for himself</u>'.

Writer's Technique

When the audience <u>know more</u> about something than the character on stage, it's called <u>dramatic irony</u> (see page 50).

Analysis of Act One — The Inspector Begins

An inspector calls and says a girl has died

1) The Inspector gives a <u>blunt account</u> of Eva Smith's <u>death</u>.

2) The <u>harsh language</u> — "Burnt her inside out" — <u>contrasts</u> violently with the <u>polite</u> and <u>playful</u> atmosphere at the start. The Inspector <u>catches</u> the Birlings <u>off-guard</u>, which helps his investigation.

3) The Inspector shows a photograph to Birling but <u>doesn't show it</u> to either <u>Gerald or Eric</u>. This is important because Gerald later suspects that each person was shown a <u>different photograph</u>, believing it to be the same one.

> **Theme — Family Life**
>
> The Birlings' family life is held together by <u>secrets</u> and <u>polite behaviour</u>. The Inspector <u>disrupts</u> everything and lets the secrets out.

Birling sacked Eva Smith to protect his business

KEY EVENT

1) The Inspector gets Birling to <u>tell the story</u> of why he sacked Eva Smith. This gives Birling a <u>false sense</u> of <u>being in charge</u> for a bit.

2) The workers at the Birling factory <u>went on strike</u> after Birling refused a pay rise. He wanted to protect his profits and prevent another strike, so he <u>sacked</u> the "ring-leaders", including Eva Smith.

3) This story gives the play a <u>political element</u>. Priestley's positioning the <u>rights</u> of the <u>workers</u> against the <u>interests</u> of the <u>businessman</u>.

4) Eva's described as a "<u>lively good-looking girl</u>". She's remembered as an <u>attractive hero</u> — this makes Birling <u>look worse</u>.

> **Theme — Social Responsibility**
>
> Birling sees employees as "<u>cheap labour</u>". If he can get them to work for less, he will do. He wants the opposite of 'social responsibility' — maximum <u>profit</u> for the <u>individual</u>.

Then Sheila got her sacked from her next job

KEY EVENT

Photo: An Inspector Calls, ©2010 Lamb's Players Theatre

1) Sheila's shown a <u>photograph</u> — possibly <u>not the same</u> one that Birling saw. She recognises the woman she got <u>sacked</u> from Milwards last year.

2) Sheila's <u>insecurity</u> and <u>jealousy</u> made her think that Eva Smith was <u>laughing</u> at her at Milwards.

3) As a <u>regular customer</u> from a <u>good family</u> she had the power to demand that Eva Smith be sacked from her job. Sheila <u>abused</u> her <u>influence</u>.

4) But Sheila also says she "felt rotten about it at the time", and her <u>reaction</u> to the Inspector's news shows that she knew she <u>behaved badly</u> and that she's <u>grown up</u> a bit since then. Priestley portrays Sheila as a <u>forgivable</u> character.

EXAM TIP

Talk about the change of mood once the Inspector arrives...

It'll impress the examiner if you mention that the play's mood dips after the doorbell rings. Priestley sets things up nicely for the arrival of the Inspector — things can't get any better, so they must get worse.

Section One — Discussion of Acts

Analysis of Act One — Eva Smith is Daisy Renton

Priestley ends Act One with the Inspector's reappearance because it makes the audience wonder how much the Inspector already knows, and how much there is yet to find out. Priestley's keeping his audience alert.

Sheila and Eric are sympathetic

1) Eric points out the <u>hypocrisy</u> of sacking Eva Smith for asking for higher wages because the Birling company "<u>try for the highest possible prices</u>."

Hypocrisy is when someone's actions don't match what they claim to believe.

2) Eric and Sheila give <u>emotional responses</u> to the Inspector's story, while their parents show <u>no sympathy</u>.

3) Sheila's repeatedly told to leave the room by both her parents — she stays because she feels it's her <u>duty</u> to stay to hear the <u>whole story</u> and to find out who's <u>responsible</u>.

> **Theme — Young and Old**
>
> The Birlings don't think a young woman should hear this grim story. However, Sheila's a <u>young woman</u> who <u>thinks for herself</u> and <u>breaks away</u> from her parents' <u>traditional</u> views.

Eva Smith changes her name to Daisy Renton

1) The Inspector explains that after being sacked from Milwards Eva Smith decided to <u>change her name</u>.

> • Perhaps Eva Smith needed a <u>dramatic change</u> to <u>escape</u> her past.
>
> • Or maybe this is just the Inspector spinning a tale to <u>link</u> two separate women.
>
> • Either way, the name Daisy Renton's a <u>fresh</u> sounding name for a fresh start. But '<u>under the daisies</u>' was a <u>euphemism</u> for being <u>dead</u> (see p.50). And '<u>renting</u>' suggests <u>prostitution</u>. Maybe the name isn't so fresh after all.

2) Gerald is "<u>startled</u>" — he recognises the name.

© WATERGATE PRODS / THE KOBAL COLLECTION

Gerald confesses to Sheila

1) Eric and the Inspector leave to find Birling, giving Sheila the opportunity to <u>question Gerald</u>.

2) Gerald says his affair with Daisy was "<u>over</u> and done with last summer". He suggests that they should <u>keep it secret</u> so that it doesn't become a scandal.

3) Sheila's sure that the Inspector <u>knows everything</u> already — she's worried about "how much he knows that we don't know yet". Gerald and Sheila get more <u>anxious</u> and <u>suspicious</u>, which heightens the <u>tension</u>.

> **Theme — Men and Women**
>
> It was <u>considered okay</u> for men to have affairs and mistresses. It wouldn't have been <u>acceptable</u> for Sheila to have a lover.

4) The Inspector <u>slowly opens</u> the door and looks "<u>searchingly</u>" as if he can read their expressions. He says only <u>one word</u> but it confirms that he's in <u>control</u> and <u>expects</u> something from them: "<u>Well</u>?"

Analysis of Act Two — Gerald's Affair

The Inspector is piecing together the events of the final couple of years of Eva/Daisy's life. Act Two starts with the Inspector questioning Gerald about how he came to know Daisy.

Gerald kept Daisy as his mistress

1) Gerald <u>ignores</u> the Inspector's question, "Well?", and <u>excuses</u> Sheila for being "<u>hysterical</u>". He's trying to get Sheila to <u>leave</u> so he doesn't have to tell her more details about his <u>affair</u>.

2) The Inspector points out Gerald's <u>hypocrisy</u> in thinking that women should be "<u>protected</u>" when it's men like him that took advantage of Daisy Renton — "one young woman who wasn't" protected.

3) Gerald tells the others about his affair with Daisy. He defends the relationship — "You know, it wasn't <u>disgusting</u>", but Mrs Birling is <u>shocked</u>. She doesn't understand the term "<u>women of the town</u>" (prostitutes) and is upset to learn that Gerald's been seeing them.

> **Theme — Men and Women**
>
> If the Palace stalls are well known for being a place to pick up <u>prostitutes</u>, it's likely Gerald went there to find a prostitute himself.

Daisy fell in love with Gerald out of gratitude

1) Sheila suggests that Daisy loved Gerald as her "<u>wonderful Fairy Prince</u>". Gerald doesn't say he loved Daisy, but agrees that he "adored" being <u>loved</u> by her.

2) Gerald <u>finished</u> with Eva/Daisy just before he went on a business trip. Although he gave her some money, he effectively made her <u>homeless</u>.

3) Eva/Daisy went to a "seaside place" to remember their time together "just to make it <u>last longer</u>". For Gerald, it was a summer fling, but for Eva/Daisy "there'd <u>never</u> be anything as good <u>again</u>".

Gerald is shamed and Sheila breaks off the engagement

KEY EVENT

© Simon Gough Photography

> **Theme — Learning about Life**
>
> Although she's dazzled by the ring at first, Sheila's <u>mature</u> enough to realise the <u>consequences</u> of marrying a man who has <u>lied</u> to her.

1) Gerald should have confessed all this <u>months ago</u>. Less than an hour ago he said he hadn't seen Sheila much last summer because he was too busy at work. He <u>lied</u>.

2) Sheila says they'd "have to start <u>all over again</u>, getting to know each other".

3) Birling <u>defends</u> Gerald, saying, "you must understand that a lot of young men —". He implies that <u>lots of men</u> have mistresses.

4) Gerald doesn't ask Birling for permission to leave. He <u>asks</u> the Inspector. This shows that the Inspector's in <u>control</u> now, and not Birling.

EXAM TIP

Mention the different characters' opinions of the affair...

Gerald's revelation doesn't shock Birling — he thinks it's OK for a man to have a mistress — but Sybil thinks it's "disgusting". Men and women in the play seem to have different opinions on what's acceptable.

Analysis of Act Two — Sybil Refused to Help

Priestley wants to show how lies underpin this family's life. Gerald's been lying about last summer, and Sybil's trying to avoid telling the truth. The fact that they're lying shows they know they've done wrong.

Sybil Birling is a hard nut to crack

1) The Inspector presents Sybil with the photograph. She pretends she doesn't <u>recognise</u> it.

2) Even when the Inspector manages to press the story out of her, Sybil won't accept <u>responsibility</u> for her actions.

3) Sybil can't <u>imagine</u> herself in a <u>similar situation</u> to Eva/Daisy — she can't <u>empathise</u>. Sybil is so obsessed with social class and reputation that she can't recognise <u>connections</u> between her life and anyone else's.

> **Theme — Young and Old**
>
> The Inspector increases the <u>tension</u> between the <u>parents</u> and <u>children</u> by using Sheila's help to get Sybil to tell the whole story.

Sybil had the last chance to help but she refused

KEY EVENT

1) Mrs Birling persuaded the committee to <u>turn down</u> Eva/Daisy's request because:

   - Eva/Daisy said her name was "Birling". Mrs Birling thought it was a "piece of <u>gross impertinence</u>" (rude) for Eva/Daisy to dare to associate her own scandal with the Birling family name.

   - She changed her story. At first she said her husband had <u>left her</u> and she was <u>pregnant</u>, but later admitted she <u>wasn't married</u>.

2) Priestley contrasts Sybil Birling's attempts to preserve her reputation with Eva/Daisy's moral standards. Eva/Daisy <u>wouldn't marry</u> the father of her child and wouldn't take any more money from him because:

   - He was a "youngster — <u>silly and wild</u> and <u>drinking too much</u>".

   - The money he'd been giving to her was <u>stolen</u>.

   - He didn't <u>love</u> her.

> **Theme — Social Class**
>
> Mrs Birling dismissed Eva/Daisy's story as "<u>ridiculous</u>" because she couldn't believe that a girl of "<u>that sort</u>" (working class) would ever refuse money. She based her refusal on <u>class prejudice</u>.

Sybil won't take responsibility

1) After trying to <u>resist</u> all the Inspector's questions, Mrs Birling realises that she can <u>blame</u> the father of the child instead of <u>admitting</u> her own guilt.

2) Sybil starts to tell everyone what she thinks should happen to <u>punish</u> this "<u>young man</u>".

3) Sybil blames the father for getting involved with a girl from a <u>different class</u>. She assumes she wouldn't know a man who <u>drinks</u> and <u>steals</u>.

4) She says that the Inspector should punish the man "<u>very severely</u>" before making him "confess in public his <u>responsibility</u>".

© Simon Gough Photography

Analysis of Act Two — Sybil Blames the Father

Mrs Birling really puts her foot in it

1) While Sybil is blaming the father of the child, the Inspector doesn't intervene, but instead lets her walk straight into a trap — demanding that he punish her own son.

2) This is the most dramatic result of questioning each person separately — Sybil answers the Inspector's questions, totally unaware of what Eric is going to say.

3) But Sheila is open to the idea that her family are guilty and guesses that Eric might well be the "young man" that Sybil's determined to blame.

© Simon Gough Photography

Sheila quickly sees what's going on

1) If the audience already think that Sheila has matured since the incident at Milwards, they realise that she's now a very different Sheila from the well-behaved and blushing bride-to-be of Act One.

2) Sheila can be determined and stubborn like her parents. But while her parents use their stubbornness to resist the Inspector, Sheila's stubbornness leads her to seek out the truth.

3) Sheila demands that Gerald and Sybil answer the Inspector's questions and tells Birling not to interfere when he's defending the behaviour of young men sleeping around.

Themes — Learning about Life

She recognised that she'd changed when she handed the ring back to Gerald, saying that they weren't "the same people who sat down to dinner".

Perfectly on cue — Eric walks in

KEY EVENT

Turning point in the action
All the major characters (except Gerald) are now on stage. Eric is forced to give a public confession.

© Alastair Muir/Rex Features

1) Eric walks in, looking "*extremely pale and distressed*". It's as if he has been summoned to the dock, and his mother's already declared him guilty without knowing.

2) Eric's been absent for much of the play. He left the dining room in Act One and even left the house earlier in Act Two. Eric is always running away from his family and their expectations of him.

3) Act Two finishes with a cliffhanger. The audience is left wondering whether or not Eric was the "drunken young idler" that got Eva/Daisy pregnant.

KEY QUOTE

"No, he's giving us rope — so that we'll hang ourselves."

Sheila's smart — she realises pretty quickly that the Birlings are all going to walk straight into the Inspector's trap. Mrs Birling dismisses her as over-excited, but she soon regrets not listening to what Sheila's saying...

Section One — Discussion of Acts

Analysis of Act Three — Eric Confesses

The Inspector just had to open the cracks in the Birling family, and it's broken apart. Priestley carefully engineered the plot so that once the ball got rolling, the family just started to self-destruct.

Eric confesses all — and it's a bit of a mess

1) Eric's <u>ready</u> to <u>confess</u>. He's guessed that the Inspector's helped everyone realise he's the father of Eva/Daisy's child — "<u>You know, don't you?</u>".

2) Eric explains that he forced Eva/Daisy to have sex with him, and got her pregnant — he was so <u>drunk</u> he threatened to cause a "<u>row</u>" if she didn't let him in to her flat.

3) He <u>regrets</u> his <u>actions</u>, but his <u>language</u> shows his immaturity. Eric calls Eva/Daisy "<u>a good sport</u>" and "<u>pretty</u>" — this sounds <u>insensitive</u> given how badly he treated her. Eric says that she treated him as a "<u>kid</u>".

4) Eric doesn't understand how middle-class men are <u>supposed</u> to behave. His parents think he's acted <u>worse</u> than Gerald, who knew how to have an <u>affair</u> without creating a <u>scandal</u> — but it makes the audience start <u>blaming</u> his <u>parents</u> for his upbringing.

Birling's appalled — not by suicide, but by theft and shame

1) Arthur Birling starts to take the situation <u>seriously</u> for the first time. His son's <u>stolen money</u> from the company to help support Eva/Daisy.

2) In the middle of Eric's story Arthur orders the <u>women</u> to <u>leave</u>.

3) Eric's involvement has gone <u>too far</u> for the Birling family. He'd have had an <u>illegitimate child</u> with a <u>prostitute</u>. This would have brought <u>shame</u> on the family.

Sybil returns and brings Eric bad news

1) Sybil and Sheila return to the dining room because Sybil "had to <u>know</u> what's happening" — she disobeys her husband now she realises how involved she is in the story.

2) Because Eric's been <u>outside</u>, he hasn't heard that Sybil was <u>involved</u> in Eva/Daisy's and his child's <u>death</u>. When he finds out he's furious, and links her failure to "<u>understand</u>" to his own <u>childhood</u> — "You don't understand anything. You never did."

Some productions, such as Stephen Daldry's (as seen above), emphasise Sybil's reaction to discovering her role in her grandchild's death.

Themes — Family Life

Sybil's kept a polite household and a perfect <u>reputation</u> for the family, but at the <u>cost</u> of a <u>close</u> and <u>understanding</u> relationship with her children.

Turning point in the action

Every member of the family has let down their defences. They're primed and ready for the Inspector's speech...

Analysis of Act Three — The Inspector's Speech

The Inspector has his say

KEY EVENT

1) First, the Inspector <u>sums up</u> how <u>each person</u> at the dinner party <u>played their part</u> in Eva/Daisy's short life:

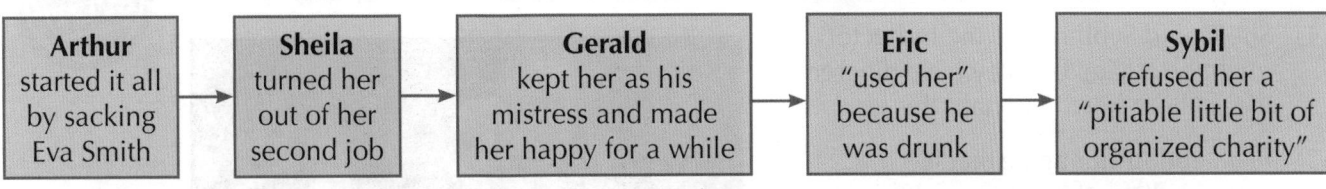

Arthur started it all by sacking Eva Smith	**Sheila** turned her out of her second job	**Gerald** kept her as his mistress and made her happy for a while	**Eric** "used her" because he was drunk	**Sybil** refused her a "pitiable little bit of organized charity"

2) Now that the Inspector has broken through their <u>defences</u>, they're ready to hear his message.

- He <u>links</u> Eva/Daisy to the "millions of Eva Smiths and John Smiths" — the <u>rest of society</u>, or even the <u>rest of humanity</u>.

- He says everyone is "<u>intertwined</u>" and "<u>members of one body</u>" — everyone <u>shares</u> "their hopes and fears, their suffering and chance of happiness" because <u>everyone's affected</u>.

- He warns that if people don't <u>learn</u> to be more <u>responsible</u>, they'll be forced to understand their mistakes through "<u>fire and blood and anguish</u>". The Inspector's foreseeing all the <u>suffering</u> that will result from <u>selfishness</u>, including the <u>world wars</u>.

The Birling family structure collapses

1) The Inspector tells them at the start of Act Three that they'll have plenty of time to "<u>adjust</u>" their family <u>relationships</u>.

2) The first words after the Inspector's exit are Birling <u>blaming</u> Eric for their problems. This signals a <u>decline</u> from the Inspector's <u>moral speech</u> into <u>petty squabbling</u>.

3) Arthur Birling doesn't want anything to change. He's <u>desperate</u> to get things back to <u>how they were</u> — with him <u>in charge</u>.

© Simon Gough Photography

Everyone's ashamed — but not necessarily of themselves

Themes — Learning about Life

Birling says he's "<u>learnt plenty</u>", but not about how and why he's been wrong. He's learnt how Sheila and Eric <u>really behave</u> and <u>think</u>, and he's not impressed.

1) The word "<u>ashamed</u>" is passed between the family members. First <u>Sybil</u> tells Eric she's "absolutely ashamed" of his <u>drinking</u>.

2) <u>Eric</u> then says he's ashamed of his <u>parents' actions</u>.

3) Finally, <u>Sheila</u> says that she's ashamed of her <u>own actions</u>. She <u>shoulders the blame</u>, and asks everyone else to do the same.

4) The parents <u>haven't learnt anything</u>. They're more focused on trying to keep all the revelations <u>in the family</u>. The only thing they'd feel ashamed of is a <u>scandal</u>.

KEY QUOTE

"We don't live alone. We are members of one body."

The play's coming to a close — it's usually time for the characters to learn their lessons. The Inspector does his best to make this happen, but not all of the Birlings are prepared to take responsibility for their actions.

Analysis of Act Three — Was it a Hoax?

Just when you think you've got it all worked out, there's a big twist. Apparently, Inspector Goole doesn't even exist — how do you explain that one? Then a final phone call tells us that there'll be no neat, happy ending...

The Inspector might not have been a real inspector

1) Sheila and Sybil realise the Inspector might be a <u>fake</u>, but they have different ideas about how important this is.

2) Sybil and Arthur agree that it makes "<u>all the difference</u>" if it wasn't a real police visit.

3) Sheila and Eric disagree — "He was <u>our police inspector</u> all right". It doesn't matter if the Inspector was <u>fake</u> if what he's shown them is true.

Photo: An Inspector Calls, ©2010 Lamb's Players Theatre

KEY EVENT

Gerald's return splits the family further

1) Gerald returns and says that he's found out there's <u>no Inspector Goole</u> on the force. Birling calls the police station to confirm that Goole wasn't a real inspector, and starts to think of the night's events as a <u>hoax</u>, with himself as the <u>victim</u>.

2) Sybil starts to <u>rewrite</u> her role in the evening — she says she's <u>proud</u> that she "didn't give in to him".

3) Gerald points out that the photograph might have been <u>different photographs</u> of <u>different girls</u>. Gerald calls the hospital and confirms that there's been no suicide — Birling is very relieved and considers himself <u>guilt-free</u>.

4) Gerald tells Sheila "<u>Everything's all right now</u>" while offering her the ring. She says it's "<u>too soon</u>" to be thinking about that and <u>forgetting</u> all she learnt this evening.

5) Gerald and Mr and Mrs Birling are relaxed and joking. The <u>atmosphere</u> seems just like it did at the start of the play — it's almost like a <u>happy ending</u>.

Writer's Technique

Priestley gives Gerald the <u>role</u> of a <u>detective</u> at the end of a <u>murder mystery</u> — he pieces together the events and <u>summarises</u> it for the others. But instead of <u>solving</u> the crime, Gerald makes it seem as if there was <u>no crime</u> at all.

A phone call... a girl has died, and an inspector will call

This news arrives with the same <u>spooky accuracy</u> as the Inspector's first arrival:

1) The Inspector first arrived <u>just after</u> Birling had said that "<u>a man has to mind his own business</u>". The Inspector's message was all about <u>social responsibility</u>.

2) And at the end of the play the phone rings <u>just after</u> Birling has <u>laughed</u> at "the famous younger generation who know it all". Birling still thinks <u>he knows it all</u> — he's <u>not learnt</u> the Inspector's lesson.

EXAM TIP
Mention the way different characters react...

There's a split in the way the characters react to the news that the Inspector isn't who he seemed. Mention that the elder Birlings and Gerald are relieved to get off scot-free — but Sheila and Eric still feel guilty.

Section One — Discussion of Acts

Practice Questions

So, by now you should know 'An Inspector Calls' pretty well, and be able to pick out important moments and details to help you analyse the plot. Try answering these quick questions in a line or two to make sure.

Quick Questions

Act One

1) How does the opening scene suggest that the Birlings are the 'perfect' family?

2) Before the Inspector arrives, Arthur Birling makes a speech about the state of the world. Name one event that the audience know will happen after 1912 which prove he's wrong.

3) Explain in your own words why Arthur Birling sacked Eva Smith.

4) Why does Eric disagree with his father's decision to sack Eva Smith?

5) Explain in your own words why Sheila Birling got Eva Smith sacked.

6) Give two reasons why Priestley would have Eva Smith change her name to Daisy Renton.

Act Two

1) What word finishes Act One and begins Act Two?

2) How does Sheila react towards Gerald once he has finished telling his story?

3) Give one piece of evidence which suggests that Gerald's bad behaviour was quite common among middle-class men of the time.

4) Give two reasons why Sybil refused to help Eva/Daisy.

5) Who does Sybil say is ultimately the one responsible for Eva/Daisy's death?

6) Why does Sheila suspect that Eric might be the "young man" who got Eva/Daisy pregnant?

Act Three

1) Give two examples of language that Eric uses which suggests he's immature.

2) What piece of news makes Eric turn on his mother?

3) Summarise the Inspector's final speech in three main points.

4) Explain how each of the four family members react to his speech.

5) Why do the characters start to think that the Inspector might have been a fake?

6) Three telephone calls are made in Act Three. Say who makes each call, and what is revealed.

Practice Questions

Feel like you're in the play — pretend that I'm the Inspector and I'm giving you a good grilling.
Ah hello. May I come in? I've got a few questions for you. Yes, it concerns a certain play...

In-depth Questions

1) Think about your first impressions of Sheila in Act One.
   What sort of character did you expect her to be?

2) Do you think the Inspector planned to leave Sheila and Gerald alone together
   at the end of Act 1? How do you think this might benefit his investigation?

3) Mrs Birling persuaded her charity to refuse to help Eva/Daisy. In your own words,
   explain why she might have done this.

4) The Inspector questions Mrs Birling before he questions Eric. What do you think would
   have happened if Eric had still been in the room when Mrs Birling was explaining her
   role in Eva/Daisy's death?

5) Priestley puts 'cliffhangers' at the end of each act in the play.
   How do these sudden endings affect the audience?

6) Why do you think the Inspector leaves so abruptly after giving his final speech?

7) Why do you think Priestley adds the final twist, rather than ending
   the play with the discovery that there was no suicide victim?

8) Copy out the graph below. Draw a line that best represents the building of tension levels
   following these key events in the plot:

a)	Inspector's arrival	b)	Gerald's confession	c)	Eric's return
d)	Inspector's speech	e)	Gerald's 'theory'	f)	The final phone call

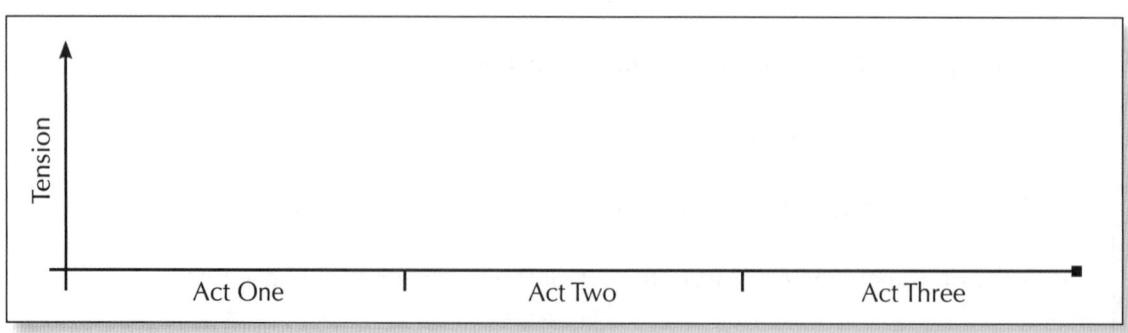

Practice Questions

You've read the play, you've answered the questions, you've got the T-shirt... Sadly the actual exam questions are likely to be a bit more challenging than the quick questions, so here are some practice exam-style questions so you know what you'll be up against.

Exam-style Questions

1) Look at Act One, from where Birling says "All right, Edna. Show him in here." to Eric's line "My God!" and answer the following question.
   How does Priestley create a change in mood and tone in this passage?

2) 'From the very beginning of the play, there are already signs of what is to come.'
   Do you see the beginning of the play in this way? How does Priestley prepare the audience for the Birlings' downfall?

3) What is the significance of the title *An Inspector Calls*?

4) 'The Inspector's descriptions of Eva Smith's death are unnecessarily graphic.'
   How effective is the Inspector's language in presenting Eva Smith's life and death, and to what extent do you think his descriptions are necessary?

5) In Act Three, Eric admits his involvement in Daisy Renton's death.
   He says "The fact remains that I did what I did."
   How does Priestley present Eric as a forgivable character in Act Three?

6) Discuss the way that Priestley uses entrances and exits in Act Three of *An Inspector Calls*. Think carefully about how certain characters affect the order of events.

7) Discuss how Priestley uses the play's structure to build tension and increase the audience's curiosity. Use evidence from the text to support your answer.

8) Look closely at Sheila's confession in Act One and the way she talks to her parents in Act Three. How does Priestley change the way Sheila is presented over the course of the play? Remember to use examples from the text to back up your answer.

Character Profile — The Inspector

At the end of the play it's not clear who or what the Inspector was. This uncertainty makes a big difference to some of the Birlings, but not to others. "Who was he?" and "Why did he 'call'?" are very different questions...

The Inspector "massively" takes charge

1) The Inspector arrives <u>unexpectedly</u>. He just says he's here to ask some questions.

2) He's an <u>outsider</u>. He doesn't seem to have much in common with the Birlings.

3) The Inspector leaves after delivering a speech about <u>social responsibility</u>. When Gerald finds out that the Inspector is probably a <u>fake</u>, the older characters <u>forget</u> his speech and try to avoid the blame.

4) He is described as <u>authoritative</u> and <u>imposing</u>. He's not a big man — but his presence <u>fills the room</u>.

Photo: An Inspector Calls, ©2010 Lamb's Players Theatre

Inspector Goole is...

Moral: "We don't live alone. We are members of one body"

Authoritative: "All in good time"

Mysterious: "Was it a hoax?"

An outsider: "The rude way he spoke to Mr Birling and me — it was quite extraordinary!"

The Inspector is the driving force of the play

Think of the Inspector as the <u>engine</u> of the play — he keeps things rolling by <u>asking pushy questions</u>:

1) He starts it all off with a <u>summary</u> of the afternoon's events — "Suicide, of course."

2) He <u>forces</u> more information out of people by <u>bluntly</u> saying what the other characters try to <u>skirt around</u> — e.g. When Gerald's describing how he met Daisy Renton, the Inspector asks "And then you decided to keep her — as your mistress?" But it's <u>not really a question</u>. This forces Gerald to admit the <u>truth</u>.

3) He also <u>reveals new information</u> which <u>heightens</u> the <u>drama</u>, such as when he drops it into the conversation "that this girl was going to have a child".

The Inspector's 'calling' is pretty ominous

1) The word "calls" sounds so <u>casual</u> — as if he's just dropping in.

2) "Calls" is a <u>deceptive</u> word to use about the Inspector. He may appear casual and spontaneous, but in fact he's <u>single-minded</u> and <u>calculating</u>. If anything, he 'calls' the shots.

3) Another inspector "<u>calls</u>" the Birling household on the <u>telephone</u> at the end of the play.

4) The title of the play is <u>echoed</u> in Edna's words as she announces the arrival of Inspector Goole at the <u>start of the play</u> and in the telephone call at the <u>end of the play</u>.

Character Profile — The Inspector

His language is emotive and personal

1) Inspector Goole has come to the house to stir things up. He does this with <u>emotive language</u>.

2) He describes Eva/Daisy as a "<u>pretty</u>" and "<u>lively</u>" girl. These <u>attractive words</u> make the audience more <u>sympathetic</u> towards her.

3) This sympathy is strengthened by the <u>harsh tone</u> used to describe her death. He says that she's now lying "with a <u>burnt-out inside</u> on a slab".

4) Sheila is "*<u>rather distressed</u>*" by the Inspector's language and says that she "can't help thinking about this girl — <u>destroying</u> herself".

© Donald Cooper/Rex Features

The Inspector uses shock tactics

1) He <u>answers</u> his <u>own questions</u> if he's not happy with someone's answer — e.g. when Sybil <u>refuses</u> to admit there was a committee meeting he says, "You know very well there was, Mrs Birling."

2) He follows up questions with <u>more questions</u> until he has pieced together a <u>confession</u> — e.g. when Sybil won't say she <u>convinced</u> the committee to reject Eva/Daisy's appeal he asks "Was it or was it not your <u>influence</u>?"

3) He's <u>blunt</u>, "You're not even sorry now, when you know what happened", and is prepared to ask <u>personal questions</u> — e.g. he asks Gerald "Were you in <u>love</u> with her?".

Writer's Technique

Priestley makes the Inspector's language <u>forceful</u> and <u>to the point</u> — he forces the other characters to <u>answer</u> him.

He knows how to make an entrance — and an exit too...

1) The Inspector's timing's <u>crucial</u>. Priestley has the Inspector ring the bell just as Arthur says "a man has to mind his own business". It's as if Birling's announcement summons the Inspector to prove the <u>exact opposite</u>.

For more about entrances and exits see page 48

2) The Inspector <u>uses exits</u> as a <u>clever tactic</u>. Leaving Sheila and Gerald alone lets Sheila <u>interrogate</u> Gerald and allows the time for <u>suspicion</u> to break them apart. This makes it <u>easier</u> to get Gerald to confess when the Inspector returns.

3) The Inspector's language gets more <u>dramatic</u>, which builds on the <u>tension</u> and <u>emotion</u> of the final scene. He claims that if the Birlings don't learn their lesson, they will be taught it in "<u>fire and blood and anguish</u>."

4) After his last exit there's a sudden <u>silence</u> because no one else has been speaking. The audience, like the characters on stage, are left "<u>staring, subdued and wondering</u>".

EXAM TIP

Write about the use of stage directions...

Show that you've paid attention to the whole text by mentioning stage directions. Priestley uses them to describe the Inspector. His authoritative voice and "impression of massiveness" get everyone under his spell.

Character Profile — The Inspector

Inspector Goole — quite the mystery man. Is he an Inspector? Is he even a man? The audience know by the end that he "definitely wasn't a police inspector at all". But they don't ever find out what he actually was.

Whooo is this Inspector Ghoul?

1) At the end of the play, the audience aren't sure <u>who</u> or <u>what</u> the Inspector is.

2) He claims he found "<u>a rough sort of diary</u>" kept by Eva/Daisy. But her <u>identity</u> isn't certain, and the audience aren't sure she ever <u>existed</u> (see p.32-33). So, the diary might be a neat <u>bluff</u> to stop anyone asking *him* any questions.

> **Writer's Technique**
>
> It's a bit of a joke that Inspector Goole's name sounds like '<u>Ghoul</u>' — a word for 'ghost'. Priestley's put little clues into some of the character's names (see Eva/Daisy on p.8 and p.33).

3) Why he has so much knowledge and power is never properly explained. He could be a <u>ghost</u>. Or he could represent the <u>spirit</u> of a <u>religious</u> or <u>moral</u> figure — just like in the Medieval morality plays (see p.42).

He's more than a police inspector

1) In a way, he represents the <u>police</u> and the <u>courts</u> — he's tracking down the truth, like in a murder mystery.

2) Because he's not a police officer, Mr and Mrs Birling don't think he has the <u>authority</u> to tell them off.

3) Eric and Sheila realise that his <u>moral judgement</u> is just as important as his legal power.

4) Goole has the attitude of a <u>philosopher</u> and <u>social commentator</u>, and the knowledge of a spooky ghost delivering a <u>prophesy</u>.

© Paul Lovelace/Rex Features

His authority strengthens his strong moral tone

1) Whatever Goole is, his <u>unsettling presence</u> might just be down to <u>confidence</u>. He knows how to create an <u>air of uncertainty</u> and reel everyone in.

> **Writer's Technique**
>
> It's worth thinking about how an actor might play the Inspector — maybe with his voice getting <u>louder and louder</u> as the play progresses.

2) He makes sure everyone recognises that he's <u>in charge</u>.

3) He takes control and leads the events. They're confused, but Goole <u>never</u> is.

4) He "massively" interrupts which means that he cuts into the dialogue "<u>with authority</u>", e.g. when he tells Birling that Eric can "wait his turn".

5) His <u>authority</u> makes people take him <u>more seriously</u> and makes everything he says sound more <u>important</u>.

Character Profile — The Inspector

The Inspector's from a different world

The Inspector doesn't share Arthur Birling's interests or values:

> 1) The Inspector doesn't play golf and he's <u>not impressed</u> by Arthur Birling's public profile as former Alderman and Lord Mayor.
>
> 2) He talks about <u>taboo subjects</u> like sex and politics.
>
> 3) He interrupts, repeats and pauses in ways which were not the norm in middle-class prewar England. He <u>doesn't follow etiquette</u> (normal rules of social behaviour).

For more about etiquette see p.24.

The Inspector is classless

1) The Inspector seems to come from <u>outside</u> the <u>class system</u> that the Birlings live in. This makes him '<u>classless</u>'.

2) The Inspector doesn't recognise any of the Birlings' ideas about class. He treats <u>everyone</u> the <u>same</u>.

3) Instead, he says that "We are <u>members</u> of <u>one body</u>" so classes shouldn't <u>ignore</u> each other's needs.

Theme — Social Class

Priestley has set his play in the Birlings' <u>dining room</u>. In 1912 only well-off households would have had a dining room — this makes it a <u>symbol</u> of the <u>middle-class lifestyle</u>.

Priestley uses the Inspector as a mouthpiece

See p.44 for more on Priestley's socialist views.

J.B. Priestley

1) The Inspector stands <u>outside</u> the <u>class system</u> of the Birlings' social world — he is an outsider in the play.

2) But he <u>doesn't</u> take a <u>neutral</u> position — he's on Eva/Daisy's side, and he tells the Birlings what he thinks of them.

3) Priestley's <u>own views</u> are reflected in the opinions of the Inspector. You could say that the Inspector is Priestley's '<u>mouthpiece</u>' — Priestley's <u>voice</u> in the play.

4) This is most clear during the Inspector's final speech. He's speaking to the Birling family, but it could also be <u>Priestley's speech</u> direct to the <u>play's audience</u>.

5) The play (and Priestley) has a <u>strong message</u> about looking after one another, and it's the Inspector's job to <u>deliver</u> it.

"He never seemed like an ordinary police inspector —"

Gosh — what a pickle. Sheila admits that something wasn't right about him from the start, but nobody ever knows who or what Goole is. It does seem like he's been used as Priestley's ventriloquist puppet, though...

Character Profile — Arthur Birling

Arthur Birling's head of the Birling family. He's the boss of his own company. He even plays golf with the big shots. But he's so bothered about money and power that he can't think about anything — or anybody — else.

Arthur Birling seems to be pretty pleased with himself

1) Arthur Birling seems very <u>confident</u>. He is head of his <u>family</u> and the <u>boss</u> of his own business.

2) He likes to be in <u>control</u> and he keeps reminding everyone that he's <u>in charge</u>, e.g. Birling doesn't want to be told what to do, and "<u>angrily</u>" tells the Inspector, "Well — if you don't mind — I'll find out <u>first</u>".

3) Over the course of the play, Birling's authority is <u>undermined</u>. The Inspector reveals Birling as an <u>ambitious</u>, <u>anxious</u> man who'll <u>ignore</u> the needs of others to keep up <u>profits</u> and a <u>good reputation</u>.

© Simon Gough Photography

Birling is...

ambitious: "there's a very good chance of a knighthood"

business-minded: "a hard-headed, practical man of business"

selfish: "a man has to make his own way"

anxious: "there'll be a public scandal — unless we're lucky"

He's a successful and ambitious businessman

1) Birling hints that his company could <u>merge</u> with the larger company owned by Gerald's father. He sees his daughter's <u>marriage</u> a bit like a <u>business deal</u> and hopes it will bring "<u>lower costs</u> and <u>higher prices</u>".

2) Birling thinks he's successful because he's a "hard-headed, practical man of <u>business</u>". He has the same attitude to all areas of his life.

3) He is very <u>optimistic</u> about the future. He thinks that strikes won't be a problem for his company and dismisses any fear of <u>war</u> as just some "<u>silly little war scares</u>".

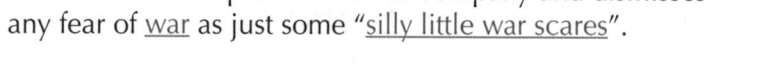

Writer's Technique

Priestley uses <u>dramatic irony</u> to make Birling's optimism seem <u>foolish</u> and <u>short-sighted</u> (see page 50). This <u>undermines</u> his authority.

He won't accept responsibility for the death of Eva Smith

Theme — Social Responsibility

Birling <u>dismisses</u> the idea of <u>social responsibility</u>. He calls people like Goole "<u>cranks</u>".

1) Birling finds it difficult to think about other people. He doesn't believe in "<u>community</u> and all that <u>nonsense</u>". He sees other people as "<u>cheap labour</u>".

2) Birling didn't just refuse higher wages for his workers — he <u>actively</u> made things worse for them. He <u>personally</u> fired the ringleaders of the strike.

3) Birling is <u>selfish</u> and <u>self-centred</u>. He'd rather pass off the Inspector's visit as a "<u>hoax</u>" or a joke than <u>face</u> up to what he's done.

Character Profile — Arthur Birling

Birling likes to be respected — he wants to be in control

1) Birling's a public figure in Brumley and obsessed with his status. When his good name's threatened he's terrified and would "give thousands" (a bribe) to avoid scandal.

2) He isn't used to being challenged. The Inspector barely says twenty words before Birling shows "*a touch of impatience*".

3) Birling's family is falling apart, and he can do nothing about it. He blames the Inspector for making a "nasty mess" of the night's celebrations.

© WATERGATE PRODS / THE KOBAL COLLECTION

Underneath it all, Birling is an anxious man

Theme — Social Class

Birling's a wealthy businessman, but it was more prestigious to come from an "old county family" like the Crofts, that had land, inherited wealth and titles (e.g. 'Lord', 'Lady').

1) Birling desperately tries to win the Crofts' approval by talking about a knighthood and by getting Gerald's father's favourite port.

2) Birling tries to make himself seem important by drawing attention to his connections with influential people — e.g. he plays golf with the Chief Inspector.

3) The Inspector threatens Birling's middle-class values — the reputation of his company, his important connections. Birling is rattled by this. He has spent his entire life believing that these things matter.

Birling uses authoritative language to be in control

Priestley uses stage directions and careful language choices to help create Birling's character:

1) Priestley writes that Birling should be "*provincial in his speech*", which means he has a regional accent. Accent and social class were closely linked, so it would be clear that Birling was a middle-class businessman rather than upper-class.

2) Birling has the most continuous speech in the play — he likes to talk and doesn't like being interrupted. When Eric tries to correct him, Birling ignores him, saying "Just let me finish, Eric".

3) Birling repeatedly shouts "Rubbish!" to dismiss what other people have said. But he finishes his own sentences with "of course", to make his own claims seem obvious and matter-of-fact.

KEY QUOTE

"*a man has to mind his own business and look after himself*"

Birling's looking after number one, and he's not going to change. He wants his business to make higher profits, but Priestley uses the character of Birling to show that this profit comes with a high moral cost.

Character Profile — Sybil Birling

Sybil's proud of her reputation and social status. She'll do anything to protect them — they're more important than the happiness of her children. Even when the Inspector's questioning her, she won't back down.

Sybil Birling is proud of her social status

Etiquette

Etiquette is a set of rules about social behaviour — what's 'acceptable' and what isn't.

1) Sybil has traditional values. She strictly follows the rules of etiquette because a good reputation for being polite will improve her family's status. These rules are more important to her than moral rules — the difference between good and bad.

2) She has a strong set of beliefs about people's social status, which makes her prejudiced.

3) To preserve her own status, she's prepared to be cruel, such as when she rejects Eva/Daisy's appeal.

© Simon Gough Photography

Sybil is...

traditional: "When you're married you'll realize..."

proud: "I was the only one of you who didn't give in to him"

prejudiced: "As if a girl of that sort would ever refuse money!"

cruel: "I used my influence to have it refused"

Sybil is Mr Birling's "social superior"

Sybil Birling is from a family with a higher social status than Arthur Birling's family. Even though Arthur's head of the family, Sybil is his "social superior":

1) Sybil tells her husband off for saying the food was good in front of a guest. It wasn't polite to mention the cook or lower servants. Upper-class families would not say "Tell cook from me".

2) Sybil's always reminding her family to have better manners — e.g. she tells Sheila off for using slang.

3) Sybil won't let anyone boss her around. She warns the Inspector, "You have no power to make me change my mind".

© WATERGATE PRODS / THE KOBAL COLLECTION

Sybil lives by strict standards

1) Sybil's social standards make her prejudiced against people from a lower class. She thinks that they have lower standards and can't imagine her son being involved with women "of that sort".

2) It's her 'standards' that make her walk straight into the Inspector's trap when he asks her who she blames for Eva/Daisy's suicide.

3) Even though it was Sybil herself who refused to help Eva/Daisy when she most needed it, she blames the father of the unborn child.

4) Without realising it, she condemns her own son and demands that he should be made to pay, and to confess publicly.

Character Profile — Sybil Birling

Sybil supports charity — but she's not very charitable

1) Mrs Birling is involved with the Brumley Women's Charity Organisation which she says only supports "deserving cases".

2) This gives Mrs Birling the authority to decide who's "deserving" and who's not.

3) She uses her "influence" (social status) to convince the other members of the board to reject Eva/Daisy's appeal because she's offended by the young woman using the Birling name.

4) She's outraged that Eva/Daisy would pretend to have the "fine feelings" of a higher social class, but Mrs Birling is unfeeling towards the women who make appeals to her.

Theme — Social Responsibility

The word "deserving" was traditionally used to distinguish between the poor who physically can't help themselves and the undeserving who shouldn't be helped.

Mrs Birling doesn't change

© Simon Gough Photography

1) Mrs Birling is self-centred. She hasn't noticed her own son's alcoholism and dismisses her daughter's worries that Gerald lost interest last summer.

2) She won't accept responsibility for her actions, and claims that she did the right thing — "I accept no blame for it at all".

3) She doesn't learn from the Inspector's message. She only regrets not having "asked him a few questions" — she wants to be in control.

Stage directions show Mrs Birling has her mind made up

Even when her language is polite, her tone is severe and superior:

1) The stage directions say that Mrs Birling answers "*haughtily*", "*very sharply*" and "*bitterly*".

2) In Act Three, Mrs Birling repeatedly tells everyone that she'd already guessed it was a hoax. The script says that she "*triumphantly*" tells everyone she knew it all along. It's more important to her that she comes out on top, than that her actions could have caused a girl's suicide.

3) In the final moments of the play, Mrs Birling is "*smiling*" and telling everyone to feel as "*amused*" as she is by the evening's events. These words suggest she has already put it all behind her.

Remember to talk about Sybil's social prejudices...

Mentioning Sybil's social prejudices will help you explain why she acts the way she does. She doesn't think Eva/Daisy's important as she's socially inferior. And at the end of the play, Sybil hasn't changed at all.

Character Profile — Sheila Birling

Sheila's not heard the old saying 'start as you mean to go on' — at the beginning of the play she seems childish and petty, but later reveals herself as thoughtful, sensitive and sharp. By the end, Sheila wants to start again...

Sheila seems to be different from the rest of her family

1) Sheila's <u>quick-witted</u> and <u>strong-minded</u>. She hands Gerald's ring back when she finds out he's been unfaithful and is wise enough to suspect that Eric might be the father of Eva/Daisy's child.

2) However, Sheila was <u>more selfish</u> the year before. She <u>abused her status</u> as a wealthy customer at Milwards when she insisted they <u>dismiss Eva/Daisy</u>.

3) Sheila is now seen to be <u>sensitive</u> and <u>moral</u>. By the end of the play, Sheila has <u>changed for good</u>.

© Simon Gough Photography

Sheila is...

Strong-minded: "I don't believe I will. So you be careful."

Sharp: "he's giving us the rope — so that we'll hang ourselves"

Selfish: "you used the power you had [...] to punish the girl"

Moral: "But these girls aren't cheap labour — they're *people*"

Sheila's language makes her seem childish at first...

1) The stage directions say she's "*very <u>pleased with life</u> and <u>rather excited</u>*".

2) She uses slang expressions like "<u>squiffy</u>" which remind the audience that Sheila belongs to a <u>younger generation</u>.

3) When she gets the ring she's very <u>excited</u>, and looks to her mother for <u>approval</u> when she says "Look — <u>Mummy</u> — isn't it a beauty?".

4) She <u>jokes</u> with Gerald, but the stage directions say that she's "<u>half serious, half playful</u>". Her childishness might be a way to hide "<u>serious</u>" concerns about her relationship with Gerald.

Writer's Technique

Priestley gives Sheila lots of <u>witty lines</u> to make her appear sharp. Sheila's <u>wit</u> lets her <u>undermine</u> the <u>authority</u> of the others as she makes jokes at their expense.

...but Sheila's more mature than the audience first think

Sheila behaves childishly at the beginning, but what she <u>learns</u> over the evening makes her feel she has to be herself and break away from her parents.

1) She has <u>wise</u> instincts — she sees what the Inspector is doing, and knew Gerald's absence was <u>suspicious</u>.

2) She's <u>not naive</u> — she knows men use <u>prostitutes</u> and knows about <u>dirty old men</u> like Alderman Meggarty.

3) As the Inspector says, she "<u>isn't living on the moon</u>", and as she says to her father, "<u>I'm not a child</u>."

© Donald Cooper/Rex Features

Character Profile — Sheila Birling

Sheila has moral standards

1) Sheila acknowledges she used her "power" to "punish" Eva Smith, but she regrets her actions and is eager to <u>learn</u> from the <u>consequences</u>.

2) Priestley uses her as a moral judge at the end of the play — she says "probably between us <u>we killed her</u>." The others don't get as far as admitting that.

3) She tells Gerald she respects him more for being "<u>honest</u>". She also knows the family must <u>stop</u> these "<u>silly pretences</u>". Priestley uses Sheila to show there's <u>hope</u> for <u>change</u> in the new generation.

Theme — Learning about Life

Priestley makes Sheila seem young and <u>childish</u> at first. It makes her involvement in Eva/Daisy's downfall seem like the result of <u>immaturity</u>. This makes it <u>easier to forgive</u> her.

The Inspector's revelations change her for good

© Chesil Theatre Winchester

1) Before Gerald leaves, she <u>hands back</u> the engagement ring, saying that they are <u>changed people</u> — "You and I aren't the same people who sat down to dinner here."

2) After the Inspector goes, her parents want everything to return to the <u>way it was</u>. Sheila, along with Eric, are the only ones who see that they all <u>have to change</u>.

3) Out of <u>all</u> the characters in the play Sheila's the one who changes the <u>most</u>.

Sheila becomes a bit like the Inspector herself

It's not surprising that Sheila takes the Inspector's <u>side</u> in a lot of this, and even seems to <u>help</u> the Inspector's investigations. They're both after the <u>truth</u>. She adopts some of the Inspector's techniques:

1) She asks Gerald as many <u>questions</u> as the Inspector does.

2) She <u>reveals</u> Eric's <u>drinking problem</u> to her mother.

3) She <u>contradicts</u> and <u>undermines</u> her parents, like the Inspector does. When she's giving the ring back to Gerald she tells her father, "<u>Don't interfere</u>".

4) She <u>shocks</u> Eric by telling him that his mother <u>refused</u> to <u>help</u> Eva/Daisy. The Inspector <u>moves</u> the discussion on quickly by suddenly <u>startling</u> the listeners, and Sheila does the same.

Sheila sees that the Inspector <u>attacks</u> the others' confidence by asking questions. He does this to break down the "wall" which they've put between <u>themselves</u> and the girl — Sheila wants to do the same.

Write about how Sheila's character develops...

Sheila offers hope to the audience — she grows up by the end of the play and realises she needs to change her priorities. Explain in your essay that she allows the Inspector's story to affect and change her.

Character Profile — Eric Birling

Eric is a troubled soul. He has turned away from his family and taken up drinking. But no one seems to notice, or at least they think it's more polite to not mention it. So, instead, Eric's friendless and stuck.

Eric Birling is a troublesome son

1) Eric's <u>isolated</u> from the rest of his family. He says that <u>no one understands</u> him and he doesn't feel as if he can talk to any of them.

2) Eric apparently forced himself on Eva/Daisy while he was <u>drunk</u> and got her <u>pregnant</u>. He was so drunk he didn't even remember it happening.

3) Eric deeply <u>regrets</u> his actions — by the end of the play he says he'll <u>never forget</u> what he has learnt.

Eric is...

Irresponsible: "I didn't even remember — that's the hellish thing"

Unloved: "You don't understand anything. You never did."

Sensitive: "My God — I'm not likely to forget"

An alcoholic: "I was in that state when a chap easily turns nasty"

Priestley drops hints that Eric isn't all right

1) Priestley's stage directions say that Eric is "*not quite at ease*". He's described as being "*half shy*" and "*half assertive*".

2) He <u>interrupts</u> Sheila and Gerald when he "*suddenly guffaws*", but says he doesn't know why he's laughing. He finds things his family say funny, even when there's <u>no joke</u>.

3) When Gerald says, "Unless Eric's been up to something," Eric acts <u>suspiciously</u> and <u>seriously</u> — "I don't think it's very funny," he says "*still uneasy*", and also answers "*defiantly*".

Writer's Technique

Priestley uses Eric's <u>odd behaviour</u> to hint that his secrets will <u>later disrupt</u> and threaten the Birlings' whole <u>way of life</u>.

Eric's been hiding some dirty secrets

Eric's <u>drunkenness</u> and <u>bad behaviour</u> represent the <u>dark side</u> of family life.

1) He's a <u>heavy drinker</u>, and has been for a while. You can see his "*familiarity with <u>quick heavy drinking</u>*" in the way he pours his whisky in Act Three. The rest of the family sees it too.

2) He got a prostitute <u>pregnant</u> — his first encounter with Eva/Daisy results in her getting <u>pregnant</u> and there's a suggestion that he <u>forced</u> himself on her.

3) He has <u>stolen money</u> from his father's business to support her.

These secrets are <u>potential dynamite</u> — if they got out and became public gossip, then Birling's knighthood, Sheila's marriage and the <u>whole family's reputation</u> could be blown sky high.

Character Profile — Eric Birling

Eric's not the only one...

1) Eric meets Eva/Daisy at the stalls bar, which is exactly where <u>Gerald</u> met her, when he was looking for <u>prostitutes</u>.

2) Birling's '<u>respectable</u>' friends go to the stalls bar to find women. The Alderman, Meggarty, even assaults young women in the town hall. They're all behaving <u>badly</u>. But no one says <u>anything</u>.

3) It's a pretty <u>murky world</u> that these 'respectable' men inhabit. The play suggests Eric's behaviour is normal for a <u>middle-class man</u>.

Two finely dressed upper-class (not always) gentlemen.

... but he's the only one to have serious consequences

1) Eric's behaviour was <u>not unusual</u> — lots of men were doing the same... just in <u>secret</u>. Eric <u>lacks self-control</u> so his secret gets out.

2) His parents don't want a <u>scandal</u>. They don't care about him as much as they care about what <u>other people</u> will think of them.

3) Eric's laugh <u>interrupts</u> the <u>polite conversation</u> earlier in the play. It's the same when his behaviour <u>disrupts</u> the polite middle-class <u>illusion</u> of <u>respectability</u>. They're all <u>keeping up appearances</u> — but Eric's making it <u>obvious</u> that there's something murky underneath.

Theme — Judgement

Gerald treats Eva/Daisy as his "mistress" and ends the affair — his <u>reputation</u> is <u>not damaged</u>. But Eric <u>drunkenly</u> gets Eva/Daisy <u>pregnant</u>, <u>steals</u> money for her and brings a <u>scandal</u> on his family.

Eric is a villain and a victim

Theme — Family Life

Birling seems <u>disappointed</u> in his son, and gets on better with Gerald. This must be a <u>crushing blow</u> for Eric.

1) Eric feels <u>isolated</u> and <u>unsupported</u> — he's had to find comfort elsewhere.

2) He shouts at his mother — "You <u>don't understand</u> anything. You never did. You never even tried —" and perhaps he's right. But he's really <u>yelling</u>. It might be the <u>angriest moment</u> in the play.

3) He's the obvious villain of the piece, but he accepts <u>responsibility</u> for what he did — "the fact remains that I did what I did". He criticises his parents for <u>pretending nothing's happened</u> — "You lot may be letting yourselves out nicely".

KEY QUOTE

"the fact remains that I did what I did."

At first, it seems clear that Eric has the lowest morals of all the characters. But then he regrets his mistakes and learns from them. He comes the furthest — the audience start to see him in a more sympathetic light.

Character Profile — Gerald Croft

Gerald's the son-in-law Mr Birling dreamt of. He's the son of the competition, Croft Limited. His mother's a Lady. He's respectable. So, apart from the secret mistress, he's spot on.

Gerald Croft is an eligible bachelor

1) At the start, Gerald seems like a good catch. He gets on well with Mr Birling and impresses Sybil Birling.

2) But then it turns out Gerald's been lying — he confesses that he had a fling with Daisy Renton last summer. Sheila hands his engagement ring back.

3) Gerald leads the Birlings to realise that Inspector Goole was not a police officer, and that there was no suicide recorded at the hospital. He sides with Mr Birling, focusing on how to protect their reputation.

Photo: An Inspector Calls, ©2010 Lamb's Players Theatre

Gerald is...

Respectable: "the easy well-bred young man-about-town"

Upper-class: "landed people and so forth"

A liar: "I wasn't telling you a complete lie"

Traditional: "I should say so!" (Gerald agreeing with Birling)

Gerald's got a rosy future ahead of him...

Gerald's got a lot going for him. He's handsome, wealthy, about thirty — a respectable man-about-town.

1) He's from an old county family — unlike the Birlings. That makes him their social superior.

2) Gerald works for 'Crofts Limited'. This is his father's firm, and is older and bigger than 'Birling and Company' — the two companies are "friendly rivals". He'll probably take it over when his father retires.

3) He's relaxed and comfortable in this company (unlike Eric), and shares jokes with Birling.

... but it's a future that looks an awful lot like Birling's

Gerald's like a younger version of Arthur Birling. He's used to and comfortable with being in control.

1) Gerald agrees with Birling on politics and women and laughs at his joke about getting into trouble.

2) He supports Arthur's sacking of Eva Smith — "You couldn't have done anything else."

3) He's business-minded and is committed to his work in the same way that Arthur Birling is.

4) He and Arthur are the ones who are determined to take action at the end to find out whether the Inspector or the girl were real.

Theme — Young and Old

If it wasn't for Gerald, it'd be easy to say that Mr and Mrs Birling are selfish and unchanging because they're too old. But Gerald's character shows that younger people can be just as selfish and old-fashioned.

Character Profile — Gerald Croft

Gerald's language shows he doesn't feel sorry for his actions

Priestley makes Gerald sound <u>less passionate</u> than Sheila. Gerald can <u>distance</u> himself from the tragedy.

1) He's the <u>first character</u> to use the word "<u>hoax</u>" — he's very keen to prove the Inspector was a <u>fake</u> and clear everyone's names.

2) At the end of the play, he says "<u>Everything's all right</u> now, Sheila" to comfort her. He doesn't seem to have learnt any lessons.

© Simon Gough Photography

He thinks he's done nothing wrong

Theme — Social Class

Gerald might have made Eva/Daisy <u>happy</u> for a time, but he still <u>treated her badly</u> because of her <u>social status</u>. He kept her as a mistress for his own <u>pleasure</u> and discarded her when it suited him.

1) Gerald says that Eva/Daisy "didn't blame me at all". Perhaps the audience <u>don't blame Gerald</u> much at first because <u>Eva/Daisy didn't</u>.

2) The Inspector isn't too harsh on him because Gerald "had some <u>affection</u> for her and made her happy for a time". Gerald had some <u>positive effects</u> on Eva/Daisy's life.

3) But then he <u>left her</u> and went off on a business trip. He effectively made her <u>homeless</u>.

Gerald's not simply bad or good

This is a <u>difficult</u> one. Priestley's made it hard to see Gerald as simply good or bad. He's a complex character.

1) Gerald is confident but he's also <u>stubborn</u> — he doesn't learn much about himself over the course of the play. The Inspector points out Gerald's <u>hypocrisy</u>:

- The Inspector asks Gerald whether he thinks "young women ought to be <u>protected</u> against <u>unpleasant</u> and <u>disturbing</u> things?". Gerald says yes, thinking of Sheila.

- <u>But</u> it's people like Gerald who are <u>doing</u> the unpleasant and disturbing things to women like Eva/Daisy — he uses her and then <u>discards</u> her. This applies just as much to Mr Birling and <u>other men</u> like him who have the <u>same attitudes</u>.

2) Gerald has the ability to <u>separate</u> his <u>public</u>, <u>respectable image</u> from <u>secret</u>, <u>private acts</u> — something Eric doesn't get the hang of.

"Everything's all right now, Sheila."

Gerald was upset when he learnt that Eva/Daisy was dead — but he's gotten over it already. He won't let a fake inspector play a prank on him. Not when he's got a reputation to maintain, and Sheila to win back.

Character Profile — Eva Smith / Daisy Renton

Who was Eva Smith? No idea. Were Eva Smith and Daisy Renton the same person? Was she even real? No idea. What matters most is what Eva/Daisy represents, and what she means to the Birlings.

Who was Eva Smith?

1) Eva Smith was one of Arthur Birling's employees, who was <u>sacked</u> for <u>protesting</u> against <u>lower wages</u>. This dismissal is the first in a <u>chain of events</u> that sees the Birling family tied up in Eva Smith's death.

2) According to the Inspector, Eva Smith changes her name to Daisy Renton and becomes a <u>prostitute</u>, which is how she meets Gerald and Eric.

3) The <u>real identity</u> of Eva/Daisy is <u>never revealed</u>. She could be the <u>same person</u>, or <u>different people</u> who are treated as <u>the same</u> by the Birling family. They see one working-class girl as being the same as another.

©iStockphoto.com/Ian McDonnell

Eva/Daisy is...

Attractive: "young and fresh and charming"

Honourable: "she didn't want to take any more money from him"

Working-class: "Girls of that class", "a girl of that sort"

A Prostitute: "There was some woman who wanted her to go there"

The Birlings take away all of Eva/Daisy's sources of income

1) <u>Factory worker</u> at Birling and Company — she was a good worker but Birling sacked her for <u>speaking up</u>.

2) <u>Shop assistant</u> at Milwards — Sheila got her sacked out of <u>jealousy</u> for Eva/Daisy's good looks.

3) <u>Prostitute</u> and <u>mistress</u> to Gerald — he rescued her from the life of a <u>prostitute</u> but <u>dropped</u> her when it <u>suited</u> him.

4) <u>Prostitute</u> — she can't <u>make a living</u> this way after Eric forced her to have sex and got her <u>pregnant</u> while he was drunk.

Theme — Social Class

Eva/Daisy lost <u>all</u> these forms of <u>support</u> because other people used their <u>power</u> to move her on or have sex with her. Each of them felt <u>superior</u> to Eva because of their social class.

She never sought revenge, so the Inspector does it for her

1) Priestley has made Eva/Daisy a <u>silent</u>, <u>offstage</u> character, so in the play she represents the <u>silent</u>, <u>invisible</u> and <u>powerless</u> members of <u>society</u>.

2) Maybe Eva/Daisy didn't feel that she had the <u>power</u> to make life difficult for the people who mistreated her. She was <u>trapped</u> by her situation.

3) Inspector Goole <u>speaks</u> for Eva/Daisy and uses her as a <u>symbol</u> of the powerless working class to teach the Birlings about <u>social responsibility</u> and to make them realise their <u>mistakes</u>.

Theme — Social Class

Some productions of *An Inspector Calls* put Eva/Daisy <u>on stage</u>, sometimes as a <u>ghost</u>.

Character Profile — Eva Smith / Daisy Renton

Were Eva Smith and Daisy Renton the same person?

1) Gerald claims there were lots of <u>different</u> girls — "We've no proof it was the <u>same photograph</u> and therefore <u>no proof</u> it was the <u>same girl</u>."

2) But Gerald also says that Daisy Renton told him about having to leave a "job in one of the works here" after a strike and "something about the <u>shop</u> too" — so Eva Smith <u>must</u> be Daisy Renton. But...

- The <u>phone call</u> at the end of the play confuses everything. Has Eva/Daisy just committed suicide? Was the Inspector a <u>ghost</u> come to tell the <u>future</u>?

- Or is this a phone call about a <u>different</u> girl? The Inspector warned that everyone's lives are "<u>intertwined</u>", so the Birlings don't know how many lives they have affected.

- Priestley makes sure that, even if you think you've sussed it, that phone call <u>breaks up</u> the girl's <u>identity</u> again.

Photo: An Inspector Calls, ©2010 Lamb's Players Theatre

Eva Smith is a sort of everyman

<u>The identity of Eva Smith</u> is a kind of jigsaw portrait of an <u>ordinary</u> <u>working-class girl</u>, only you don't know if the pieces fit.

1) Take her first name. "Eva" — a bit like <u>Eve</u>, the first woman (so the Bible says) and <u>symbolic</u> of all women.

2) Take her second name — Smith. It's a very <u>common</u> last name, and it's from the word for a <u>tradesman</u>.

3) <u>That's it</u> — Eva Smith represents all <u>ordinary</u>, <u>working-class women</u>.

Eva Smith is central to the play's message

1) The Inspector says that there are "<u>millions</u> of <u>Eva Smiths</u> and <u>John Smiths</u> still left" and that their chances of happiness are "intertwined with our lives".

2) This is the key point — the Inspector is telling the Birlings, and the audience, to behave <u>responsibly</u> towards others.

3) So, although the focus of the <u>drama</u> is the group of five people sitting around the dining table at the beginning, the focus of the <u>play</u> is the life and death of an <u>unidentified</u> and <u>unseen</u> woman. If they all met <u>different</u> girls, it doesn't matter. Eva/Daisy is a <u>mix</u> of all the people they've ever <u>treated badly</u>.

EXAM TIP

Think about the message that Eva/Daisy conveys...

It's useful to say that Priestley uses Eva/Daisy as a way to show his audience how everyone is responsible for one another. He wanted people to realise that everything they do could affect someone else.

Practice Questions

Congratulations — that's another section done. As a special reward for your hard work, here's a trophy and a huge cake. Oh no, sorry, it's two pages of practice questions. Well, don't spend too long on these quick and in-depth questions — just use them to warm up for the next page. What a treat.

Quick Questions

1) Give two examples of how the Inspector manages to unsettle Mr Birling.

2) Summarise the message of the Inspector's speech in one sentence.

3) Find three stage directions that show how the Inspector is supposed to talk and look.

4) Give an example of how Arthur tries to impress the Inspector.

5) In one sentence, describe how Sheila comes across at the beginning of the play.

6) Name three ways in which Sybil and Sheila are different from each other.

7) Which character first suggests that the photograph is key to finding out Eva/Daisy's true identity? What does this character say about the photograph?

8) Find a quote to show that Eric regrets his actions.

9) Give two reasons why Gerald Croft is seen to be socially superior to the Birlings.

10) How did each of the Birlings affect the life of Eva/Daisy?

In-depth Questions

1) Who or what is the Inspector? Do you think that Priestley wants us to know?

2) At the start of the play, Birling is in control. When and how do you think the balance of power shifts from Birling to the Inspector?

3) If you were in charge of costume design for *An Inspector Calls*, how would you dress Mr Birling and the Inspector? You can sketch out an idea or write a paragraph explaining why you chose these costumes.

4) Do you think Sheila and Gerald should get married? Why do you think this?

5) Do you think Mrs Birling learns anything from the Inspector's visit? Use quotations from the text to back up your answer.

6) Both Eric and Gerald have relationships with Eva/Daisy. What do you feel about the way each man behaves towards her?

7) For much of the play, the younger generation (Sheila and Eric) hold different views from the older generation (Mr and Mrs Birling). Whose views does Gerald share? Find some quotations to back up your answer.

8) Explain the symbolism of Eva Smith's name and how this fits in with her role in the play.

Practice Questions

Now for the biggies. You should be practiced, warmed-up and raring to go. Write your answers to these as if they're the real thing — imagine you're sitting in the exam hall, chewing the end of your pen, and you've got a side or two of paper to fill for each question. But don't fret — they're not the real thing. It's time to practise.

Exam-style Questions

1) 'The main character in *An Inspector Calls* is never even on stage.'
   Write about how Priestley presents the character of Eva Smith/Daisy Renton?

2) 'The Birling family are presented as a close and happy family at the beginning of the play, but are left broken by the end.'
   How far do you agree with this assessment of the presentation of the Birling family?

3) Which character is the most responsible for the death of Eva/Daisy?
   Use details from the play to explain your answer.

4) "Everything's all right now, Sheila. [*Holds up the ring.*] What about this ring?"
   How does Priestley present the changing relationship between Sheila and Gerald over the course of the play?

5) 'The Inspector's an outsider — he comes in from the outside and turns the Birling family inside out.'
   What is the role of the Inspector in the play and how does Priestley use him to carry the play's message?

6) 'Sybil is perhaps the most unsympathetic character of them all.'
   How does Priestley present the character of Sybil Birling to the audience during the play?

7) 'The Birling family don't seem to consider Gerald's affair to be as shameful as Eric's relationship with Daisy Renton.'
   Does Priestley's portrayal of Gerald encourage the audience to feel more sympathetic towards Gerald than Eric?

8) 'No character in *An Inspector Calls* is entirely good or bad. This is what makes them so complex.'
   How does Priestley's portrayal of the Birlings suggest that they are flawed but have potential to change?

Section Three — Context and Themes

Britain in 1912 and 1945

An Inspector Calls is set near the beginning of the 20th century. Priestley wrote it in the 1940s. You're reading it now at the beginning of the next century. How things have changed...

In 1912 Britain was a very different place from how it is now

1) British society was firmly <u>divided</u> along <u>class</u> lines. Those with the <u>most money</u> had the <u>most power</u>. The <u>Labour Party</u> was formed in 1906 to represent the <u>interests</u> of the working class.

2) Only men who owned <u>property</u> could vote. <u>Women</u> weren't allowed to <u>vote</u> in national elections at all. Women's lives were far <u>more controlled</u> by their families and husbands than today.

3) There was not as much government help for people in need as there is today. This is why <u>charities</u> like Sybil's were so <u>important</u>.

The 1912 National Miners' Strike
Over a million workers across Britain campaigned for fairer wages for miners. At the time it was the largest strike in Britain.

Britain was heading towards the First World War...

• There was a dangerous level of <u>tension</u> between the big European countries in 1912, which resulted in the First World War (1914-1918). This was a <u>terrible conflict</u> which cost <u>millions of lives</u>.

• After the war many British people <u>questioned</u> the <u>leadership</u> given by the <u>upper classes</u> during the war.

Things had changed by 1945 — but there were still big problems

1) Britain was still divided by class, but by 1928 all <u>men</u> and <u>women</u> over <u>21</u> got the <u>vote</u>, which meant <u>power</u> was shared out more <u>evenly</u>.

2) There were still conflicts between business owners and workers, such as the 1926 <u>General Strike</u> which saw many important <u>industries</u> grind to a halt.

3) From 1930 a <u>global economic slump</u> known as the <u>Depression</u> hit many British industries. There was a big increase in <u>unemployment</u> and many workers faced terrible <u>poverty</u>.

Priestley wrote the play during the Second World War

• <u>Millions</u> of people from all classes had <u>fought</u> for Britain during the Second World War (1939-1945). After the war people wanted to work out how to make a better <u>society</u>.

• The world wars made people <u>question</u> Britain's <u>social structure</u>. <u>Socialism</u> and other <u>left-wing</u> ideas, which call for the more equal sharing out of wealth and power, became more <u>popular</u>.

Right-wing ideas favour private ownership and wealth.

• The <u>Labour Party</u> won the 1945 General Election by a landslide. In government they focused on improving the <u>welfare system</u> to look after the needs of the <u>poorest</u> in British society, e.g. the NHS was started in 1948.

Talk about why Priestley set the play when he did...

Mention that a lot changed in British society between 1912 and 1945. Priestley set the play at the start of the 20th century to show that things had improved, but he also highlights that many things had not.

Family Life

At the start, Gerald thinks that the Birlings seem to be "a nice well-behaved family". But Gerald, and the audience, are yet to find out about the murky secrets lurking behind their polite and polished behaviour.

There were expectations of middle-class families in 1912

1) Family members were expected to <u>know their role</u>, and be <u>content</u> with their <u>position</u> — the parents were <u>in charge</u> of the family, and the children were expected to be <u>obedient</u> and <u>unquestioning</u>.

2) '<u>Gender roles</u>' (how men and women are supposed to behave) were well <u>defined</u> for the <u>wealthy middle class</u>:

Men were expected to:	Women were expected to:
• Work to <u>support</u> their '<u>perfect</u>' family. • <u>Protect women</u> — especially their wives and daughters.	• <u>Marry</u> into money so they didn't have to work. • Plan <u>parties</u>, visit <u>friends</u> and <u>have children</u>. They didn't do jobs like <u>washing</u>, <u>cooking</u> or <u>cleaning</u>.

3) However, <u>working-class</u> families, and especially working-class <u>women</u>, had very different roles. Many had <u>jobs</u> in factories or worked as servants.

The Birling family seems fairly normal...

1) The Birlings want everyone to <u>believe</u> they're the <u>perfect family</u>.

2) The <u>gender roles</u> are clearly <u>defined</u> — the ladies 'withdraw' to let the men talk about 'male' stuff.

3) But there's <u>tension</u> bubbling just under the surface:

Photo: An Inspector Calls, ©2010 Lamb's Players Theatre

> • Mrs Birling keeps correcting her family's <u>social mistakes</u>.
>
> • Eric laughs out of turn and acts <u>oddly</u>.
>
> • Sheila <u>teases</u> Gerald half playfully, but also "*half serious*", about last summer.

... but something's not right

1) The clear <u>hierarchy</u> at the beginning is <u>destroyed</u> by the Inspector's arrival.

2) Without their parents' influence, Sheila and Eric can <u>think for themselves</u>:

A hierarchy is a way of ranking people according to status or authority.

> • Sheila doesn't know whether she'll marry Gerald any more. She needs time to decide for herself.
>
> • Eric says his mother doesn't "<u>understand anything</u>" and that Birling's "not the kind of father a chap could go to" for help.
>
> • The family is in a <u>mess</u>, and Sheila and Eric <u>refuse</u> to "<u>go on behaving just as we did</u>". They don't want to <u>pretend</u> any more. The parents no longer have any <u>authority</u> over their children.

KEY QUOTE

"You seem to be a nice well-behaved family —"

The Birling family is held together by lies, and when the truth's revealed they fall apart. And it's not pretty. There's hatred, envy, theft, prostitutes, and even being responsible for the death of your own grandchild...

Social Class

Social class is really important in *An Inspector Calls*. Class influences the Birlings' behaviour and causes them to treat people differently. The class system had existed for a long time and Priestley didn't agree with it.

Class drives the plot and shapes the characters

Photo: An Inspector Calls, ©2010 Lamb's Players Theatre

1) Priestley <u>designed</u> the characters to put across his <u>message</u>.

2) The message is about <u>social responsibility</u>, so class plays a <u>central part</u> in the plot.

3) The characters in the play <u>represent</u> the classes — and Priestley challenges their <u>views</u> and <u>behaviour</u> in order to challenge the <u>class hierarchy</u>.

There was a clear class structure in the early 20th century

Many things contributed to what class you were in, but most of it came down to <u>money</u> — those who had it, and those who didn't. There were <u>three</u> main classes:

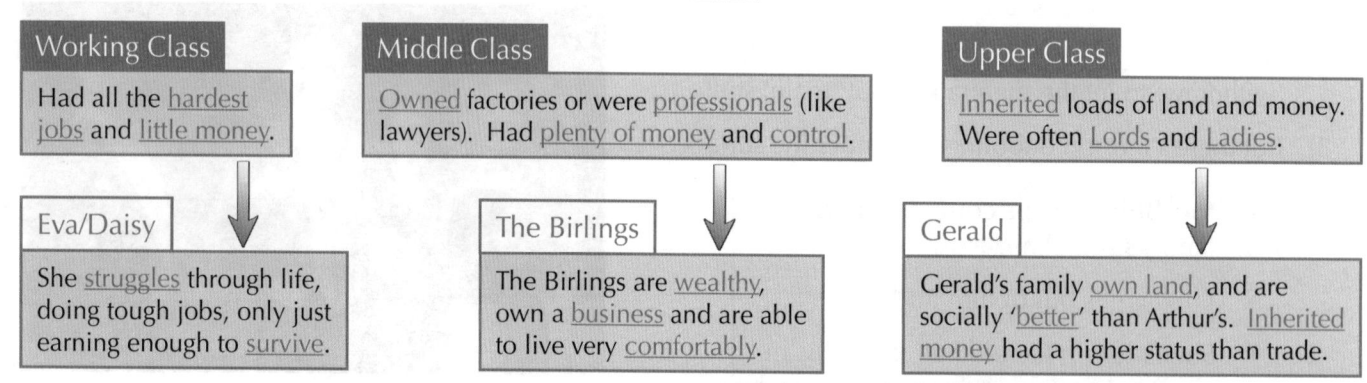

Working Class

Had all the <u>hardest jobs</u> and <u>little money</u>.

Eva/Daisy

She <u>struggles</u> through life, doing tough jobs, only just earning enough to <u>survive</u>.

Middle Class

<u>Owned</u> factories or were <u>professionals</u> (like lawyers). Had <u>plenty of money</u> and <u>control</u>.

The Birlings

The Birlings are <u>wealthy</u>, own a <u>business</u> and are able to live very <u>comfortably</u>.

Upper Class

<u>Inherited</u> loads of land and money. Were often <u>Lords</u> and <u>Ladies</u>.

Gerald

Gerald's family <u>own land</u>, and are socially '<u>better</u>' than Arthur's. <u>Inherited money</u> had a higher status than trade.

The class system meant the lower classes struggled

1) The class system could make life <u>difficult</u> for those lower down — it would have been hard for people like Eva/Daisy to help themselves if they were in <u>trouble</u>.

2) Priestley portrays the upper classes as having a <u>limited</u> sense of <u>social responsibility</u> for those less well off. They either:

> DIDN'T KNOW   OR   DIDN'T WANT TO KNOW   OR   DIDN'T CARE

3) Mrs Birling claims not to recognise Eva/Daisy's photo. For her, Eva/Daisy has <u>no identity</u>.

4) Priestley suggested that the higher classes didn't question the class system as it <u>worked</u> for them. This is the same reason why they also <u>overlooked</u> problems of <u>alcoholism</u> and <u>womanising</u> — it was easier to ignore unpleasant things than to deal with them.

5) The Inspector tells the Birlings that they must <u>accept</u> that everyone should take <u>responsibility</u> for each other, or it'll all end in "<u>fire</u>", "<u>blood</u>" and "<u>anguish</u>".

Social Class

The Birlings think class is all that matters

1) Birling's biggest <u>concern</u> about Eva's death is that he won't get his knighthood because there will be a "<u>public scandal</u>".

2) Birling thinks his positions of <u>authority</u> make him more <u>important</u>. He'd been <u>Lord Mayor</u> and an <u>Alderman</u> (Council member) for many years, and he's now a <u>magistrate</u> who sits in courts and dishes out justice.

3) He uses Gerald to <u>promote</u> his social class — he asks him to hint to his parents that he's expecting a knighthood, and he's also very pleased that his daughter is marrying into a <u>higher class</u>.

4) Sybil Birling is a leading member of the Brumley <u>Women's Charity Organisation</u>. This group's <u>supposed</u> to give money to desperate women, but Mrs Birling's only involved for the social <u>status</u>.

Theme — Judgement
It's ironic that Birling <u>passes judgement</u> on others when he's acted so <u>immorally</u>.

Priestley thought class shouldn't matter

1) Priestley uses the play to <u>reveal</u> the <u>unfairness</u> of the class system — he uses the Birlings as exaggerated <u>caricatures</u> of all the <u>bad qualities</u> he thought the ruling classes had.

2) The play isn't just about <u>one family's scandal</u>. It shows how Priestley saw <u>society</u>. Priestley presents the Birlings' arrogant behaviour and selfish attitudes as <u>common</u> to the middle classes.

3) Priestley presents the working class as <u>victims</u> of the <u>class system</u> — although Eva/Daisy's story is <u>unique</u>, the miseries she suffered were probably quite <u>common</u>. Eva Smith could have been <u>anyone</u>.

© Jimmy Sime/Stringer/Hulton Archive/Getty Images

How people act isn't just about class

1) Eva/Daisy is expected to have <u>low morals</u>, but she <u>refuses</u> to accept stolen money even when she's desperate.

2) The Birlings think that <u>class</u> is all that matters, but Priestley is trying to present the <u>opposite view</u>. He suggests that class only <u>clouds</u> people's <u>judgements</u>, and people should be judged by <u>what they do</u>, not by what class they happen to be in.

Writer's Technique
Priestley's presentation of Eva/Daisy as more <u>honourable</u> than the middle and upper classes might have <u>surprised</u> some members of the <u>audience</u>.

3) By presenting Sheila and Eric as having <u>changed</u> at the end of the play, <u>turning against</u> the views of their own class, Priestley's saying that class isn't all that matters — individuals can <u>break out</u> and choose to act differently.

EXAM TIP

Talk about how the Inspector doesn't have a class...

The Inspector doesn't clearly fit into the class structure, and he thinks everyone should be treated equally. You could write about how he challenges attitudes about class, and makes Sheila and Eric want to change.

Young and Old

The Inspector, and his story about Eva Smith/Daisy Renton, causes a rift between the old traditionalists and the young idealists. One side wants nothing to do with the story — the other feels like it's their job to rewrite it.

The older generation are old-fashioned

1) Priestley presents Arthur and Sybil Birling as having very traditional views — they think that they know best, that children should be seen and not heard, and they don't like their authority to be challenged.

2) They represent the views of the ruling class.

3) By questioning their old-fashioned personal views, Priestley also questions their obsession with social class — he's suggesting that the whole class system is out of touch and needs to be reformed.

The younger generation are different

1) Some are ambitious, determined and motivated — Eva/Daisy "had a lot to say — far too much". Her courage is the main reason Birling sacked her.

2) The younger generation are shown as challenging the authority of their elders. This threatens Birling, who tells them they'd "better keep quiet".

3) Because the younger generation learn their lesson, there's a chance for an equal and fairer society in the future.

Theme — Learning

Eric and Sheila learn that they are responsible for their actions and that their decisions affect other people.

Eric at the end is standing around as if he wants nothing to do with his parents. Sheila stands by him. By the end of the play they're no longer controlled by their parents.

Gerald's the oldest young man around

1) Gerald's closer to Sheila and Eric's age than he is to Mr and Mrs Birling's, but he's a young man who's already old in his attitudes. He's a younger version of Arthur — shallow and stubborn:

- His marriage to Sheila is for business reasons.

- He agrees with Birling that Eva/Daisy had to be fired.

2) He doesn't learn anything:

- When he's found out to have ditched Daisy/Eva, he doesn't seem to feel guilty.

- At the end, he thinks his engagement's back on: "Everything's all right now, Sheila."

Photo: An Inspector Calls, ©2010 Lamb's Players Theatre

3) The fact that Gerald is of the younger generation but remains unchanged suggests that a more caring future isn't inevitable — people can choose whether to change or not. Priestley is also making a criticism of the upper classes, that they're set in their ways and therefore unlikely to change.

KEY QUOTE

"the famous younger generation who know it all."

Although Birling's being sarcastic, Priestley shows that the only characters who really listen to the Inspector's message are Sheila and Eric. Mr and Mrs Birling aren't as willing to change or learn from their mistakes.

Men and Women

In 1912, men and women had different roles in the family and society — they led very different lives from each other. Priestley is asking his audience to think about how people are treated differently because of their gender.

The women and men start out as stereotypes

A stereotype is an idea you might have about people before you really know them. It's usually based on things like their sex, age and class.

WOMEN

1) They're supposed to be obsessed with "pretty clothes", shopping and weddings — Sheila gazes adoringly at her ring and asks, "is it the one you wanted me to have?".

2) They're protected against "unpleasant and disturbing" things.

3) Sheila gets Eva sacked because of pride, vanity and jealousy — stereotypical female traits in the play.

4) Sheila is accused of being hysterical — a state often associated with women at the time.

MEN

1) They're preoccupied with work and public affairs — e.g. "the miners came out on strike".

2) Gerald feels it's his duty to rescue Daisy/Eva from the womanising Alderman Meggarty.

3) Gerald is allowed to sleep around before his marriage. Sheila isn't. Arthur says that even in his day they "broke out and had a bit of fun sometimes". There are different rules for men and women.

The young women challenge the stereotypes

Eva/Daisy and Sheila try to rebel and break out of the roles that society has given them.

- Eva/Daisy questioned the decision of her boss instead of quietly accepting it.

- Instead of relying on a man to save her, Eva/Daisy refused to accept Eric's stolen money.

- Sheila interrupts and challenges everyone at different times, apart from the Inspector.

By the end the stereotypes are turned upside down

1) As the play develops Birling, Gerald and Eric get weaker, while Sheila gets stronger. Priestley does this to challenge the audience's view of women at the time.

2) Gerald's rejected by Sheila, and Eric is revealed to be nervous and lazy, with a drinking problem. Birling suffers the most — the whole night has slowly undermined his authority. He's "panic-stricken" as he speaks the final line — a very different man from the one at the beginning.

© Simon Gough Photography

3) Sheila starts stating her own opinions, not those she is 'supposed' to have — "That's what's important — and not whether a man is a police inspector or not." She's learnt to think for herself.

Mention that the Birlings judge people on their gender...

Impress the examiner by explaining how the Birlings look at class, gender and even clothes to judge people. Stereotypes help them decide who they like and don't like before getting to know them.

Section Three — Context and Themes

Judgement

Priestley makes the end of the play quite a mystery — it's a bit of a cliffhanger. Apart from making the play more exciting, it leaves the audience to figure out what has happened, and more importantly, who to judge.

The style is like an old morality play

An Inspector Calls is like a murder mystery — but it's also like a <u>morality play</u>.

1) Morality plays were <u>religious plays</u> written in the late Middle Ages. They tried to <u>teach</u> people <u>how to behave</u> and were <u>warnings</u> against the dangers of sin.

2) *An Inspector Calls* follows the <u>same kind of idea</u> as these morality plays — it <u>points</u> out everyone's <u>sins</u>, and tries to get them to <u>confess and repent</u>.

3) This play is different from the old morality plays, because it doesn't follow <u>Christian</u> ideas. The moral judge isn't <u>God</u>, it's a police inspector. Priestley makes his morality play <u>secular</u>. *Secular means 'not religious'.*

4) The Inspector represents <u>temporal law</u> (law courts not based on religion) — but in the end it turns out that it's not a legal issue — it's a <u>moral one</u>.

> **Writer's Technique**
>
> <u>Morality plays</u> focus on the <u>seven deadly sins</u> — pride, greed, lust, envy, gluttony, anger and sloth.

There's something odd about the Inspector

1) Sheila says she had an idea "<u>all along</u>" that "there was something <u>curious</u> about him" and questions the <u>supernatural</u> side of the whole thing — she asks <u>what</u> he was, not <u>who</u> he was.

2) His origin is <u>unknown</u>, and he appears <u>omniscient</u> — they didn't tell him anything he didn't already know. It seems <u>unbelievable</u> that a real inspector would know so many details. *Omniscient means 'knowing everything'.*

3) Priestley <u>deliberately</u> leaves questions about the Inspector <u>unanswered</u>, as it increases the <u>mystery</u> and the feelings of tension within the play (see p.20).

© Simon Gough Photography

The important thing is to learn the lesson

1) In the end, it <u>doesn't matter</u> who the Inspector is. He teaches the Birlings a lesson — what matters most is how they react to it and which of them learns from it.

> • Gerald, Arthur and Sybil decide it was a <u>hoax</u>. They're <u>relieved</u> that the Inspector was a <u>fraud</u> — they think they've been let <u>off the hook</u>.
>
> • Sheila and Eric <u>waver slightly</u> when they find out there was no <u>suicide</u>, but they've <u>learnt</u> the important lesson — even if their story didn't have the tragic ending it <u>might</u> have done.

2) Sheila and Eric hold true to their <u>moral instincts</u> — even when they're given an opportunity to <u>pretend</u> it never happened. The others, however, act <u>selfishly</u> and never take <u>responsibility</u> for their actions.

"You admit being prejudiced against her case?"

The final thing that doomed Eva/Daisy was Sybil's judgement that she was unworthy of charity. The Inspector reverses that process — suddenly it's Sybil, and the rest of the Birling family, who are being judged. Sneaky.

Learning about Life

This play presents a harsh world. It's not a world for innocent people. You've got to learn fast. Some innocents — like Eva/Daisy's baby — die without ever having a chance.

Some people never learn...

Theme — Young and Old

This is ironic — it's mainly the older generation who think they know it all.

1) Birling sneers at Eric's private education and the younger generation who "know it all", because he's worked his way up.

2) This arrogance is the reason why Birling is so stubborn. He doesn't think anyone has anything of use to tell him — especially not his children or a lowly inspector. He only listens to Gerald because he's from a higher social class.

3) Arthur, Sybil and Gerald's arrogance prevents them from changing. They don't see anything wrong in the way they think or act. They believe that they know best. Mr Birling's views are made clear in Act One and they don't change.

... others try to change

1) The Inspector has much more of an effect on Eric and Sheila, who are ashamed of their behaviour. They reject their parents who have refused to learn from the night's events.

2) They understand that the important thing about the evening was the lesson learnt, not whether the Inspector was real.

3) Before they even realise they're involved with the girl's death, they criticise their father's behaviour.

4) Sheila changes not only her views but also her personality — she starts out playful, self-centred and obedient, but as the play progresses her character dramatically develops and she becomes more aware, sensitive and mature.

© Simon Gough Photography

Ignorance is bliss

1) One of the reasons that the older generation refuse to change is that they're happy living in ignorance. The problems of the working class don't affect them, so they don't want to know.

2) In fact, they don't like to think about anything troubling:

   - Prostitution — "I see no point in mentioning the subject," says Birling.

   - Womanising — "you don't mean Alderman Meggarty?" says Mrs Birling, even though it's well known.

   - Drinking — "It isn't true" says Mrs Birling when Eric's habit is revealed.

3) Even Sheila tries to forget about her bad behaviour — "it didn't seem to be anything very terrible at the time."

4) They do everything they can to avoid changing, even when it's clear that they've done wrong — they refuse to believe it, and blame everyone else instead.

5) It suits them to think that they're always right — they don't see the point of changing or learning from their night's ordeal. The system works in their favour.

KEY QUOTE

"You and I aren't the same people who sat down to dinner"

Although she's no longer angry at Gerald, and respects him for finally telling the truth, Sheila knows the Inspector's visit has changed them both. She accepts her mistakes, and can't just go back to her old life.

Social Responsibility

The play's purpose is to show the importance of social responsibility — the idea that people should act in a way that helps less privileged people rather than hurting them.

The characters' views are challenged

Birling...
... thinks that community responsibility is "nonsense". The interests of business are more important than worker's rights.

Mrs Birling...
... believes that they have no responsibility to the working class — her prejudices are so ingrained that they can't be changed.

Sheila...
... realises that getting Eva/Daisy sacked out of spite was irresponsible — but she didn't do anything about it at the time. The Inspector challenges her to improve her behaviour.

Eric...
... realises too late that his selfish actions were responsible for ruining Eva/Daisy's chances of improving her life.

Social responsibility is the Inspector's main focus

1) His final speech is clear and to the point — it's a summary of his lesson about responsibility.

2) The Inspector wasn't just trying to make the family feel guilty for Eva Smith, but to make them aware of the difficulties faced by all the "millions of Eva Smiths and John Smiths".

> All the events in *An Inspector Calls* are connected. Priestley's moral seems to be that it doesn't take great people to change the world — we all change it every day just by the way we treat others.

The play reveals a lot about Priestley's socialist ideas

1) Priestley was a supporter of socialism — his plays promote social responsibility and criticise the problems caused by the class divide.

2) *An Inspector Calls* tries to make the audience question not only their social responsibility, but also how responsible they are for their own actions.

3) The audience are already wary of Birling's short-sighted opinions, so when he criticises socialism, the audience are more inclined to disagree with him. In this way Priestley uses Birling to promote socialist ideas:

- During his speech at the start, Birling says that the whole world will have "peace and prosperity" except "Russia". Russia became a socialist state in 1917, and Priestley was interested in seeing how successful this was in creating greater equality for the Russian people. The first production of *An Inspector Calls* was held in Moscow in 1946.

- Birling attacks George Bernard Shaw and H.G. Wells, who were well-known socialist writers during that time — just like Priestley in the 1940s.

Show that you understand Priestley's main message...

Priestley is a bit preachy (not surprising given his surname) but that's the point of the play. He wants to spread his ideas about social responsibility as far as he can, so show the examiner that you understand this.

Practice Questions

Priestley lived through two world wars, where people fought to defend Great Britain. With 'An Inspector Calls', he seems to be asking "What sort of society are we trying to defend?" and "Is it worth defending?". But don't worry — these quick questions aren't half as tough as that. They're just supposed to get you thinking.

Quick Questions

1) List two things that were different in 1912 compared to today.

2) What happened in 1914 that would change Britain forever?

3) List three events that changed the social structure in Britain between 1914 and 1945.

4) Which class is represented in the play by each of the following characters?
   a) Gerald   b) Arthur Birling   c) Eva Smith

5) Describe how middle-class women were expected to behave in 1912.

6) Find two quotations in the play that suggest Eric feels left out of family life.

7) List two positions of authority that Mr Birling has held.

8) How do Eric and Sheila rebel against their parents towards the end of the play?

9) What is a morality play?

10) Which other socialist writers does Priestley mention in Arthur Birling's speech about business and industry?

In-depth Questions

1) How does Priestley's presentation of the Birlings make you feel about the middle classes in 1912?

2) Does the Inspector fit into a social class? Explain your answer.

3) Joe Meggarty is an alderman and also a "notorious womanizer". What do you think Priestley is trying to say about 'respectable' society by telling us about this character?

4) At the start of the play, the characters form a clear hierarchy, with Arthur Birling at the top and Eva/Daisy at the bottom. Priestley uses the events of the play to rearrange this hierarchy. How do you think things stand at the end of the play?

5) Do you think Sheila conforms to the gender stereotype for middle-class women in 1912?

6) Why do you think the real identity of the Inspector is never revealed? Does it matter that we don't find out who he really is?

7) What effect do you think the final revelation (that a girl has died after drinking disinfectant and an inspector is on his way) will have on each of the characters?

8) As the Inspector carries out his investigation, the Birling family becomes more and more divided between the old and the young. Find some quotes which show where Gerald fits in.

Practice Questions

These theme questions are trickier than the questions about plot and characters — but this is the kind of stuff that's likely to come up in the exam, so make sure you're ready for whatever they throw at you by having a go at these exam-style questions. Always remember to use quotations from the text to back up your answer.

Exam-style Questions

1) How does Priestley present ideas about judgement in *An Inspector Calls*?

2) 'Eva Smith shows how society sees innocence as something to take advantage of.'
   How does Priestley present the theme of innocence in the play?

3) How does Priestley show the problems caused by the class system within the play?

4) How does Priestley present the idea of conflict between the generations in *An Inspector Calls*?

5) Why do you think Priestley chose to set *An Inspector Calls* in 1912?

6) Does Priestley's portrayal of Eva Smith encourage you to blame her at any point in the play?

7) 'Sheila's views on social responsibility have been permanently changed.'
   How does Priestley present the theme of social responsibility in the play?

8) How does Priestley explore the relationships between men and women in *An Inspector Calls*?

'An Inspector Calls' on the Stage

An Inspector Calls is a play — don't call it a book or a novel. Priestley wrote it for the stage — to be seen and heard and performed. These pages should help explain how to go about discussing a dramatic text.

One set can be used for the whole play

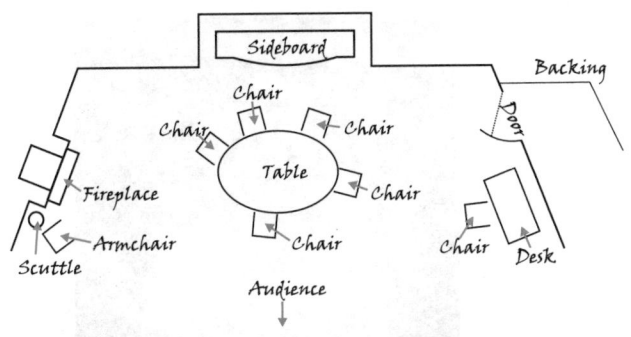

This diagram is a <u>plan</u> of the set used in the <u>first</u> production of *An Inspector Calls*, in 1946.

1) All the action takes place in the Birlings' dining room — so the <u>whole play</u> can be staged using one set (though it doesn't have to be).

2) Priestley's design helps make the <u>atmosphere</u> of the play seem more <u>claustrophobic</u> and <u>intense</u>. The room's like a kettle, just about to boil.

   A room that makes you feel trapped in a small space is described as 'claustrophobic'.

3) It emphasises the Birlings' <u>private</u> and <u>self-centred</u> lifestyle and highlights the <u>unwelcome arrival</u> of the Inspector who brings bad news from <u>outside</u>.

There are warning signs from the very beginning

1) A good production of the play should show the family <u>falling apart</u> as their secrets are revealed.

2) At the beginning the audience should see that there are <u>signs of problems</u>:

   - The actor playing <u>Sheila</u> should follow the stage directions "*half serious, half playful*" to make it clear that although she's <u>joking</u> with Gerald, she's <u>not convinced</u> he's telling her the <u>truth</u> about last summer.

   - The actor playing <u>Eric</u> needs to <u>balance</u> his <u>performance</u> as a troubled, <u>regular drinker</u>, so that he doesn't seem too <u>sober</u>, but doesn't seem too <u>drunk</u>. This <u>unsettles</u> the audience because it's clear that something's <u>not quite right</u>.

The way the play looks can say a lot about its message

1) The play takes place in <u>one room</u> — suggesting the characters have <u>closed themselves off</u> from the world, with their <u>close-minded</u> behaviour.

2) The <u>lighting</u> is "*pink and intimate*" at the start, as if the Birlings are looking through 'rose-tinted glasses'. But it becomes "*brighter and harder*" when the Inspector arrives — as if a <u>spotlight</u> is turned on their cosy world.

3) The Birlings and Gerald look <u>wealthy</u>. This should be clear from their clothes and furniture. It's part of the <u>image</u> they present to society. In <u>contrast</u>, Inspector Goole looks <u>relatively plain</u>.

4) <u>Stephen Daldry</u>'s production (first performed 1992) had an <u>unusual set</u>. The house was set on <u>stilts</u>, high above a street. The <u>height</u> showed their <u>separation</u> from the rest of the town, but the stilts made the house seem <u>unsteady</u> — suggesting that the Birlings' <u>high status</u> could easily <u>collapse</u>. Because the play wasn't just set in <u>one room</u>, the audience is reminded to think about the <u>world outside</u>.

Writer's Technique

Priestley's <u>stage directions</u> say how the play should look. But <u>productions</u> can change the <u>set</u>, <u>lighting</u> and <u>costumes</u> to suit their '<u>take</u>' on the play.

EXAM TIP

Consider how the play would be presented on stage...

Look closely at everything — from lighting instructions to set design, and even the little stage directions that say Mrs Birling speaks "triumphantly". It's all part of the play, so don't forget to talk about it in the exam.

Dramatic Techniques in 'An Inspector Calls'

Think of Priestley as an engineer — he's built the structure of the play with careful precision. He increases the tension and brings the action to an emotional climax using dramatic techniques.

Priestley paces the action to build tension and create conflict

1) At the beginning of Act Two, the audience <u>expects</u> the story to move on to Gerald's confession. But instead, Priestley <u>delays</u> the action by <u>shifting</u> the audience's <u>attention</u> to Sybil and Sheila, insisting that they should be allowed to hear what he says. This <u>builds tension</u> and <u>increases</u> the audience's <u>curiosity</u>.

2) Priestley also increases tension by having the Inspector <u>release information</u> bit by bit. He shows the photo(s) to <u>one person</u> at a time and <u>positions himself</u> so the others can't see — the characters, like the audience, are kept <u>on their toes</u>.

3) The family all start <u>seated</u>, but by the end there are people <u>standing</u>, shouting, drinking and crying — it's a dramatic but slow <u>change</u> in how the stage <u>looks</u> and <u>sounds</u>.

© Simon Gough Photography

Entrances and exits are really important

1) An exit can signal a character <u>escaping</u> someone or something — e.g. Sheila <u>runs</u> offstage when she realises she's the reason was Eva sacked. She wants to leave the <u>intense atmosphere</u> — but she's also running away from <u>telling her story</u>.

2) The Inspector uses exits to help draw <u>information</u> out of the other characters — e.g. he leaves Sheila and Gerald <u>alone</u> to discuss Daisy Renton.

3) The front door <u>bangs</u> every time someone <u>leaves</u> or <u>enters</u> the house. The characters on stage and the audience <u>hear</u> this — and wonder <u>who's</u> coming and going.

The beginnings and ends of each act are dramatic moments

Priestley <u>freezes the action</u> between Acts to create <u>tension</u>.

- Act One ends with the Inspector asking "Well?". Act Two opens with the <u>same moment</u>. The <u>audience</u> will wonder about the answer to his question during the break, which <u>builds the suspense</u>.

- The end of Act Two is another <u>cliffhanger</u>. The front door <u>slams,</u> announcing Eric's return, but Priestley makes the audience <u>wait</u> until Act Three for <u>Eric's confession</u>.

© Alastair Muir/Rex Features

Talk about the ways that Priestley creates drama...

If you just look at the plot in terms of action and events, it seems as if nothing really happens — it's just people in a room. But Priestley's dramatic techniques draw out the Birlings' stories like flashbacks in a film.

The Language of 'An Inspector Calls'

The words a character uses can say a lot about their mood or their social class. Priestley's choice of words, the director's decisions about performance and the actor's interpretation of Priestley's tone can all play a part.

The characters' language reveals more about them

The Birlings use words that were popular with middle- and upper-class people in 1912:

1) Words such as "chaps" (men) and "jingo" help show the characters' <u>social class</u>. It also suggests that the characters feel <u>comfortable</u> with each other — they're using the <u>language</u> of their <u>social group</u>.

2) Some <u>slang words</u> were popular with the <u>younger generation</u> but weren't used by their more <u>old-fashioned</u> parents. Sybil's <u>shocked</u> when Sheila says "<u>squiffy</u>".

3) Birling sees the world as a <u>businessman</u> views his company. When Birling realises the Inspector's visit was a "hoax" he uses <u>business language</u> to describe being fooled: "an elaborate <u>sell</u>!" The fact that his language links <u>sales</u> with <u>tricks</u> suggests he might not be an <u>honest</u> businessman either.

Inspector Goole uses language differently

1) The Inspector <u>doesn't mess about</u>. He <u>speaks his mind</u> — e.g. he says Eva/Daisy was burnt "inside out" by disinfectant. This contrasts with Birling's long <u>waffly</u> speech at the beginning of Act One.

© Donald Cooper/Rex Features

2) The Inspector uses <u>plain</u> and <u>direct</u> language, he only says what he <u>needs to</u> — there can't be any <u>confusion</u>.

3) He also uses <u>silence</u> — he has a "*disconcerting habit*" of staring for a while at a person before he speaks to them.

4) The older Birlings find him <u>offensive</u> because of his <u>manner</u> and <u>language</u> — he is "rude" and "impertinent".

Sheila's language changes during the play

1) At the start of the play Sheila uses <u>simple</u> and <u>childish language</u> — e.g. she says, "<u>I'm sorry, Daddy</u>," when she's admiring her ring instead of listening to her father.

2) By the end of the play she's <u>confident</u> and <u>assertive</u>. She uses <u>simple</u>, <u>plain</u> and sometimes <u>blunt English</u>, just like the Inspector — e.g. "we drove that girl to commit suicide."

> **Writer's Technique**
>
> Priestley makes Sheila's voice sound full of <u>emotion</u> — her language seems <u>honest</u> and from the <u>heart</u>.

3) She <u>directly disagrees</u> with her parents. She tells them they're <u>wrong</u> to think the Inspector was a "<u>joke</u>" and points out that they "began to learn something" before they decided it was a hoax.

KEY QUOTE

"his manner was quite extraordinary; so — so rude —"

When the Birlings are beginning to think that the Inspector might have been a fake, his attitude is the first thing that Sybil picks up on. Goole's tone and language make him stand out from the other characters.

Language Techniques in 'An Inspector Calls'

Priestley uses little language tricks to give different possible meanings to what his characters are saying. Just one carefully crafted sentence can tell the audience lots of things at once.

Priestley uses dramatic irony to influence the audience

1) It seems as if the Inspector's omniscient — he knows everything.

2) Priestley gives similar power to the audience. He set the play in 1912, but the play was first performed in 1945. The audience know that a lot of what Birling dismisses in his speech actually happened.

3) When the audience know more than the characters, it's called dramatic irony.

4) There's more irony in Act One. Birling talks about getting a knighthood unless there's a "scandal". He jokes "complacently" (as if nothing will happen) but the play's title reveals that something will happen — an inspector will call.

> **Writer's Technique**
>
> Priestley uses dramatic irony to make Birling look short-sighted (see pages 6 and 22).

The Birlings use euphemisms to hide what they mean

1) A euphemism is a way of avoiding saying something unpleasant by using other, often more vague, words.

- Eva/Daisy "went on the streets" where she led "another kind of life" with the "women of the town". These euphemisms hint that she became a prostitute.

- To Mrs Birling, Eva/Daisy is a "girl of that sort" (she means a lower-class girl), and is in a particular "condition" (pregnant).

> **Theme — Learning about Life**
>
> Part of the Inspector's message is about accepting the truth. Using euphemisms does the opposite — it covers things up.

2) The Inspector doesn't use euphemisms. His language is more direct.

The Inspector uses imagery

1) Language that creates a strong picture is called imagery.

2) The Inspector uses graphic imagery to shock — the words "Burnt her inside out" create an image that distresses Sheila and the audience.

3) The Inspector's final speech uses imagery from the Bible. This makes the Inspector sound like a religious figure:

- "We are members of one body" is an idea found in the Bible and the Inspector uses similar phrasing to suggest we have a 'sacred' duty to care for one another.

- The words "fire and blood and anguish" sound like the end of the world described in the Book of Revelation, where "fire mingled with blood" rains down — people are punished for their sins.

This cartoon from Punch magazine shows Alastair Sim, who played the Inspector in a 1954 film, as an angel with a flaming umbrella. In the Bible an angel with a flaming sword casts Adam and Eve out of the garden of Eden.

> **KEY QUOTE**
>
> ### "then they will be taught it in fire and blood and anguish."
>
> The Inspector's final speech has lots of imagery in it, because Priestley wants the audience to remember it. It's easy to get caught up in the action of the play, but don't forget to look at how language is used, too.

Section Four — The Writer's Techniques

Practice Questions

So, you've thought about the way the play looks and sounds on stage — now try your hand at some of these quick questions. Don't spend too much time answering them — and if you can't remember the answer, go back through this section to remind yourself. Then tackle the in-depth ones. They're a bit trickier.

Quick Questions

1) What is the effect of having one set for the whole play?

2) Give one example of how Priestley delays the action to build tension.

3) What are the two stage directions that show how the lighting should change over the course of the play?

4) The Birlings all start off seated and well behaved. How does this change over the course of the play?

5) Find two examples of language that reveal the speaker's social class in the play.

6) Why is it important that the front door slams every time someone comes in or goes out?

7) What does the Birlings' use of words like "by jingo" and "squiffy" say about them?

8) What is a euphemism? Give three examples of euphemisms used in *An Inspector Calls*.

9) The Inspector predicts that men will be taught their lesson "in fire and blood and anguish". What religious ideas might this be referring to?

10) Name two differences in the way that the Inspector speaks compared to the Birlings.

In-depth Questions

1) Why do you think Priestley gave stage directions about the lighting effects?

2) How does Priestley use irony for dramatic effect in the play?

3) Look at the stage directions for the Inspector in Act One. Explain the effect his actions have on the other characters.

4) Briefly sketch a set layout for a new production of *An Inspector Calls*. Explain the effect your design is intended to create.

5) Find some examples that show how Sheila's language changes during the play and explain how this changes your opinion of her character.

6) Do you think Stephen Daldry was right to extend the set design to include the street and other locations mentioned in the play? What do you think is gained and lost by this decision?

7) Why is it important that the Inspector uses powerful imagery in his final speech, while the Birlings' language tends to be more down-to-earth?

8) If you were directing a production of *An Inspector Calls*, and had decided to have Eva/Daisy on stage, what sort of costume would you choose for her? Explain your answer.

Practice Questions

Right — bring on the big guns. It's likely that you'll need to show awareness of stagecraft and the writer's techniques in your exam. Even if the exam question doesn't specifically mention it, it's good to show that you're aware of 'An Inspector Calls' as a play rather than just a story. Have a think about how the stagecraft fits in with your other ideas about the play — if you do this, you'll find these questions easy as pie.

Exam-style Questions

1) How does Priestley use stage directions to create an effect on the audience?

2) 'The difference between the Inspector and the Birlings is shown as much by how he says things as by what he says.'
   How does Priestley use language in the play to show the differences between characters?

3) Reread the play from where the Inspector says "Stop!" to where he makes his final exit.
   Explore the ways Priestley makes this such a dramatic and powerful moment in the play.

4) How does Priestley make *An Inspector Calls* such a dramatic, suspenseful play?

5) How does Priestley's portrayal of Mr and Mrs Birling contribute to the message of the play?

6) 'The characters in *An Inspector Calls* rarely say quite what they mean.'
   How does Priestley present the Birlings? Are they trustworthy in your view?

7) How does Priestley's portrayal of the Inspector make him such a powerful and moral figure?

8) 'It's clear from the start that everything is not right with the Birlings.'
   How does Priestley demonstrate this in the first part of Act One, before the Inspector arrives?

Exam Preparation

Getting to know the text will put you at a massive advantage in the exam. It's not enough just to read it though — you've got to get down and dirty with the nitty gritty bits. It's all about gathering evidence...

The exam questions will test four main skills

You will need to show the examiner that you can:

1) Write about the text in a thoughtful way — picking out appropriate examples and quotations to back up your opinions.

2) Identify and explain features of the play's form, structure and language. Show how the author uses these effectively to create meanings and effects.

3) For some exam boards, you might have to think about the play's cultural, social and historical background. Ask your teacher if you're not sure.

4) Write in a clear, well-structured way. 5% of the marks in your English Literature exams are for spelling, punctuation and grammar. Make sure that your writing is as accurate as possible.

Preparation is important

1) It's important to cover all the different sections of this book in your revision. You need to make sure you understand the text's plot, characters, themes, context and writer's techniques.

2) In the exam, you'll need to bring together your ideas about these topics to answer the question quickly.

3) Think about the different characters and themes in the text, and write down some key points and ideas about each one. Then, find some evidence to support each point — this could be something from any of the sections in this book. You could set out your evidence in a table like this:

Theme: Social Class	
Strict class structure	Rigid class structure in England in 1912. Differences between Gerald Croft, the Birlings, and Eva/Daisy.
Difficulties of being lower class	Eva/Daisy struggles to make an honest living. There are "millions and millions and millions of Eva Smiths".
Responsibility of upper and middle classes	The actions of the Birlings and Gerald cause Eva/Daisy's death. Priestley's message of social responsibility.
The Birlings' obsession with appearances	Mr Birling's concern that the scandal will lose him his knighthood. Ignoring Eric's drinking problem.
The Inspector	Not clear which class the Inspector belongs to. He challenges the Birlings' social prejudices.

Preparing to succeed — a cunning plot indeed...

Knowing the plot inside-out will be unbelievably helpful in the exam. It'll help you to stay calm and make sure you write a brilliant answer that positively glitters with little gems of evidence. The exam's just a chance for you to show off...

The Exam Question

This page deals with how to approach an exam question. The stuff below will help you get started on a scorching exam answer, more scorching than, say, a phoenix cooking fiery fajitas in a flaming furnace.

Read the question carefully and underline key words

1) The style of question you'll get depends on which exam board you're taking.

2) Read all the instructions carefully. Make sure you know how many questions you need to answer and how much time you should spend answering each one.

3) If the question has more than one part, look at the total number of marks for each bit. This should help you to plan your time in the exam.

4) Read the question at least twice so you completely understand it. Underline the key words. If you're given an extract, underline important words or phrases in that too.

Henry didn't read the weather report carefully enough when planning his weekend activities.

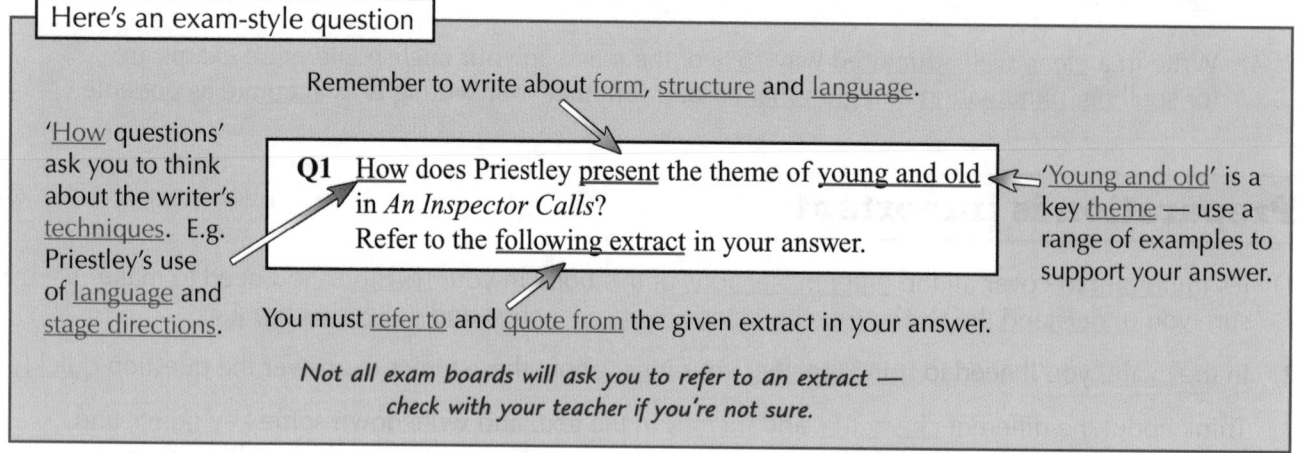

Here's an exam-style question

'How questions' ask you to think about the writer's techniques. E.g. Priestley's use of language and stage directions.

Remember to write about form, structure and language.

Q1 How does Priestley present the theme of young and old in *An Inspector Calls*?
Refer to the following extract in your answer.

'Young and old' is a key theme — use a range of examples to support your answer.

You must refer to and quote from the given extract in your answer.

Not all exam boards will ask you to refer to an extract — check with your teacher if you're not sure.

Get to know exam language

Some words come up time and again in exam questions. Have a look at some specimen questions, pick out words that are often used in questions and make sure that you understand what they mean. You could write a few down whilst you're revising. For example:

Question Word	You need to...
Explore / Explain	Show how the writer deals with a theme, character or idea. Make several different points to answer the question.
How does	Think about the techniques or literary features that the author uses to get their point across.
Give examples	Use direct quotes and describe events from the text in your own words.
Refer to	Read the question so that you know if you need to write about just an extract, or an extract and the rest of the text.

The advice squad — the best cops in the NYPD...

Whatever question you're asked in the exam, your answer should touch on the main characters, themes, structure and language of the text. All the stuff we've covered in the rest of the book in fact. It's so neat, it's almost like we planned it.

Planning Your Answer

I'll say this once — and then I'll probably repeat it several times — it is absolutely, completely, totally and utterly essential that you make a plan before you start writing. Only a fool jumps right in without a plan...

Plan your answer before you start

1) If you plan, you're less likely to forget something <u>important</u>.

2) A good plan will help you <u>organise</u> your ideas — and write a good, <u>well-structured</u> essay.

3) Write your plan at the <u>top of your answer booklet</u> and draw a <u>neat line</u> through it when you've finished.

4) <u>Don't</u> spend <u>too long</u> on your plan. It's only <u>rough work</u>, so you don't need to write in full sentences. Here are a few <u>examples</u> of different ways you can plan your answer:

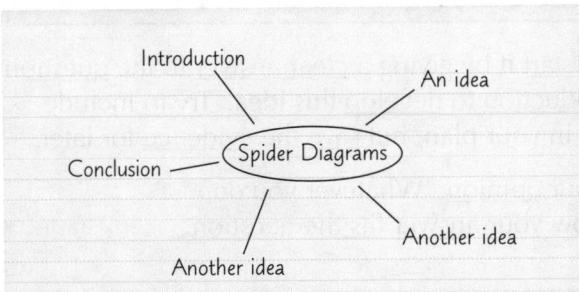

Bullet points...

- Introduction...
- An idea...
- The next idea...
- Another idea...
- Yet another idea...
- Conclusion...

Include bits of evidence in your plan

1) <u>Writing</u> your essay will be much <u>easier</u> if you include <u>important quotes</u> and <u>examples</u> in your plan.

2) You could include them in a <u>table</u> like this one:

3) <u>Don't</u> spend <u>too long</u> writing out quotes though. It's just to make sure you <u>don't forget</u> anything when you write your answer.

A point...	Quote to back this up...
Another point...	Quote...
A different point...	Example...
A brand new point...	Quote...

Structure your answer

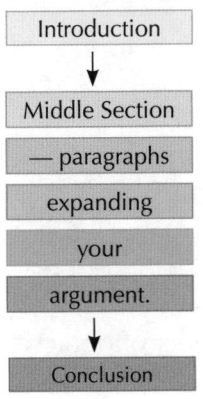

Introduction
↓
Middle Section
— paragraphs
expanding
your
argument.
↓
Conclusion

1) Your <u>introduction</u> should give a brief answer to the question you're writing about. Make it clear how you're going to <u>tackle the topic</u>.

2) The <u>middle section</u> of your essay should explain your answer in detail and give evidence to back it up. Write a <u>paragraph</u> for each point you make. Make sure you <u>comment</u> on your evidence and <u>explain how</u> it helps to <u>prove</u> your point.

3) Remember to write a <u>conclusion</u> — a paragraph at the end which <u>sums up</u> your <u>main points</u>. There's <u>more</u> about introductions and conclusions on the <u>next page</u>.

Dirk finally felt ready to tackle the topic.

To plan or not to plan, that is the question...

The answer is yes, yes, a thousand times yes. Often students dive right in, worried that planning will take up valuable time. But 5 minutes spent organising a well-structured answer is loads better than pages of waffle. Mmm waffles.

Writing Introductions and Conclusions

Now you've made that plan that I was banging on about on the last page, you'll know what your main points are. This is going to make writing your introduction and conclusion as easy as pie.

Get to the point straight away in your introduction

1) First, you need to <u>work out</u> what the question is <u>asking you</u> to do:

> ### How is the character of Sheila important to the play?
>
> The question is <u>asking you</u> to think about the <u>importance</u> of <u>Sheila</u> in the text. Plan your essay by thinking about <u>how</u> Sheila <u>links</u> to the play's <u>key themes</u>.

2) When you've <u>planned</u> your essay, you should <u>start</u> it by giving a <u>clear answer</u> to the <u>question</u> in a sentence or two. Use the <u>rest</u> of the <u>introduction</u> to <u>develop</u> this idea. Try to include the <u>main paragraph ideas</u> that you have listed in your plan, but <u>save</u> the <u>evidence</u> for later.

3) You could also use the <u>introduction</u> to give your <u>opinion</u>. Whatever you do, make sure your introduction makes it <u>clear</u> how your answer <u>fits the question</u>.

Your conclusion must answer the question

1) The <u>most important</u> thing you have to do at the <u>end</u> of your writing is to <u>summarise</u> your answer to the question.

2) It's your <u>last chance</u> to persuade the examiner, so make your <u>main point</u> again.

3) Use your <u>last sentence</u> to really <u>impress</u> the <u>examiner</u> — it will make your essay <u>stand out</u>. You could <u>develop</u> your own <u>opinion</u> of the text or <u>highlight</u> which of your <u>points</u> you thought was the most <u>interesting</u>.

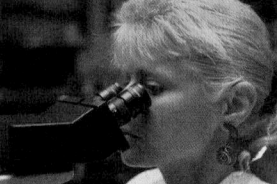

The examiner was struggling to see the answer clearly.

Use the exact question words in your introduction and conclusion

1) Try to use <u>words</u> or <u>phrases</u> from the <u>question</u> in your introduction and conclusion.

> ### How does Priestley use dramatic irony in the play?

2) <u>Repeat</u> the key words from the <u>question</u> to show the examiner that you're <u>answering the question</u>.

> Priestley uses dramatic irony in 'An Inspector Calls' to show that the character Arthur Birling is not as wise as he pretends to be, and to add humour to the play.

The first line of the introduction gives a clear answer, which will lead on to the rest of your essay.

3) This will also help you keep the question <u>fresh in your mind</u> so your answer doesn't <u>wander off-topic</u>.

I've come to the conclusion that I really like pie...

To conclude, the introduction eases the examiner in gently, whilst the conclusion is your last chance to impress. But remember — the examiner doesn't want to see any new points lurking in those closing sentences.

Writing Main Paragraphs

So we've covered the beginning and the end, now it's time for the meaty bit. The roast beef in between the prawn cocktail and the treacle tart. This page is about how to structure your paragraphs. It's quite simple...

P.E.E.D. is how to put your argument together

Remember to start a new paragraph every time you make a new point.

1) P.E.E.D. stands for: Point, Example, Explain, Develop.

2) Begin each paragraph by making a point. Then give an example from the text (either a quote or a description). Next, explain how your example backs up your point.

3) Finally, try to develop your point by writing about its effect on the audience, how it links to another part of the text or what the writer's intention is in including it.

Use short quotes to support your ideas

1) Don't just use words from the play to prove what happens in the plot...

> Sybil Birling is from a higher social class than her husband — the stage directions say that she's "her husband's social superior".

This just gives an example from the plot without offering any explanation or analysis.

2) Instead, it's much better to use short quotes as evidence to support a point you're making.

3) It makes the essay structure clearer and smoother if most quotes are embedded in your sentences.

It's better to use short, embedded quotes as evidence. Then you can go on to explain them.

> Sybil is socially "superior" to her husband, which is shown in her strict reinforcement of correct etiquette — she tells him off "reproachfully" for mentioning the servants in front of the more upper-class Gerald, for example.

Get to know some literary language

1) Using literary terms in your answer will make your essay stand out — as long as you use them correctly.

2) When you're revising, think about literary terms that are relevant to the text and how you might include them in an essay. Take a look at the table below for some examples.

Literary Term	Definition	Example
Imagery	A description that creates a strong picture.	"Burnt her inside out"
Euphemism	Avoiding saying something unpleasant by using a more vague expression.	"women of the town"
Dramatic irony	When the audience know something that a character doesn't.	"And I say there isn't a chance of war."

This page is so exciting — I nearly...

Now now, let's all be grown ups and avoid the obvious joke. It's a good way of remembering how to structure your paragraphs though. Point, Example, Explain, Develop. Simple. Maybe we could make a rap or something... anyone?

In the Exam

Keeping cool in the exam can be tricky. But if you take in all the stuff on this page, you'll soon have it down to a fine art. Then you can stroll out of that exam hall with the swagger of an essay-writing master.

Don't panic if you make a mistake

1) Okay, so say you've timed the exam beautifully. Instead of putting your feet up on the desk for the last 5 minutes, it's a good idea to <u>read through</u> your <u>answers</u> and <u>correct any mistakes</u>...

2) If you want to get rid of a mistake, <u>cross it out</u>. <u>Don't scribble</u> it out as this can look messy. Make any corrections <u>neatly</u> and <u>clearly</u> instead of writing on top of the words you've already written.

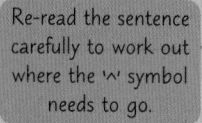
techniques
The author uses various different literary ~~teknikues~~ to explore this theme .

This is the clearest way to correct a mistake. Don't be tempted to try writing on top of the original word.

3) If you've <u>left out</u> a <u>word</u> or a <u>phrase</u> and you've got space to add it in <u>above</u> the line it's missing from, write the missing bit above the line with a '^' to show exactly where it should go.

Re-read the sentence carefully to work out where the '^' symbol needs to go.

and hyperbole
The writer uses imagery to draw attention to this point.

4) If you've left out whole <u>sentences</u> or <u>paragraphs</u>, write them in a <u>separate section</u> at the <u>end</u> of the essay. Put a <u>star</u> (*) next to both the <u>extra writing</u> and the <u>place</u> you want it to go.

Always keep an eye on the time

1) It's surprisingly <u>easy</u> to <u>run out of time</u> in exams. You've got to leave <u>enough time</u> to answer <u>all</u> the questions you're asked to do. You've also got to leave enough time to <u>finish</u> each essay properly — with a <u>clear ending</u>.

2) Here are some <u>tips</u> on how to <u>avoid</u> running out of time:

- Work out <u>how much time</u> you have for each part of your answer <u>before</u> you <u>start</u>.
- Take off a few minutes at the beginning to <u>plan</u>, and a <u>few minutes</u> at the end for your <u>conclusion</u>.
- Make sure you have a <u>watch</u> to <u>time yourself</u> — and keep checking it.
- Be <u>strict</u> with yourself — if you spend <u>too long</u> on one part of your answer, you may run out of time.
- If you're <u>running out of time</u>, keep <u>calm</u>, <u>finish</u> the <u>point</u> you're on and move on to your <u>conclusion</u>.

Stephanie never had a problem with keeping cool.

Treat an exam like a spa day — just relax...

Some people actually do lose the plot when they get into the exam. The trick is to keep calm and well... carry on. If you make sure you get your exam technique sorted, you'll be as relaxed as a sloth in a room full of easy chairs.

Sample Exam Question

And now the bit you've all been waiting for — a sample exam question and a lovely little plan.
Go make yourself a cup of tea, settle down and enjoy.

Here's a sample exam question

Read this feisty exam question. That's the best way to start...

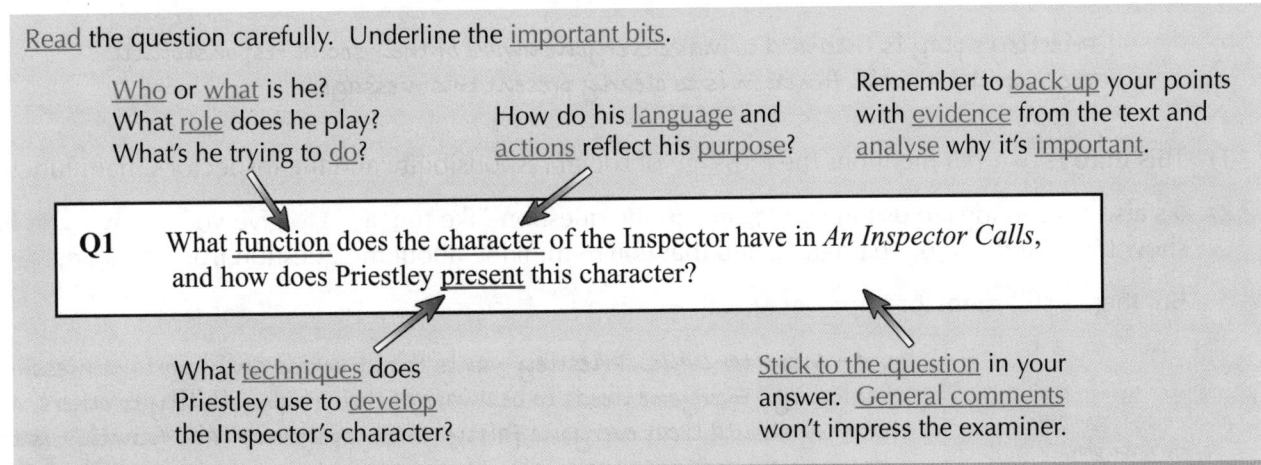

Read the question carefully. Underline the important bits.

Who or what is he?
What role does he play?
What's he trying to do?

How do his language and actions reflect his purpose?

Remember to back up your points with evidence from the text and analyse why it's important.

Q1 What function does the character of the Inspector have in *An Inspector Calls*, and how does Priestley present this character?

What techniques does Priestley use to develop the Inspector's character?

Stick to the question in your answer. General comments won't impress the examiner.

Here's how you could plan your answer...

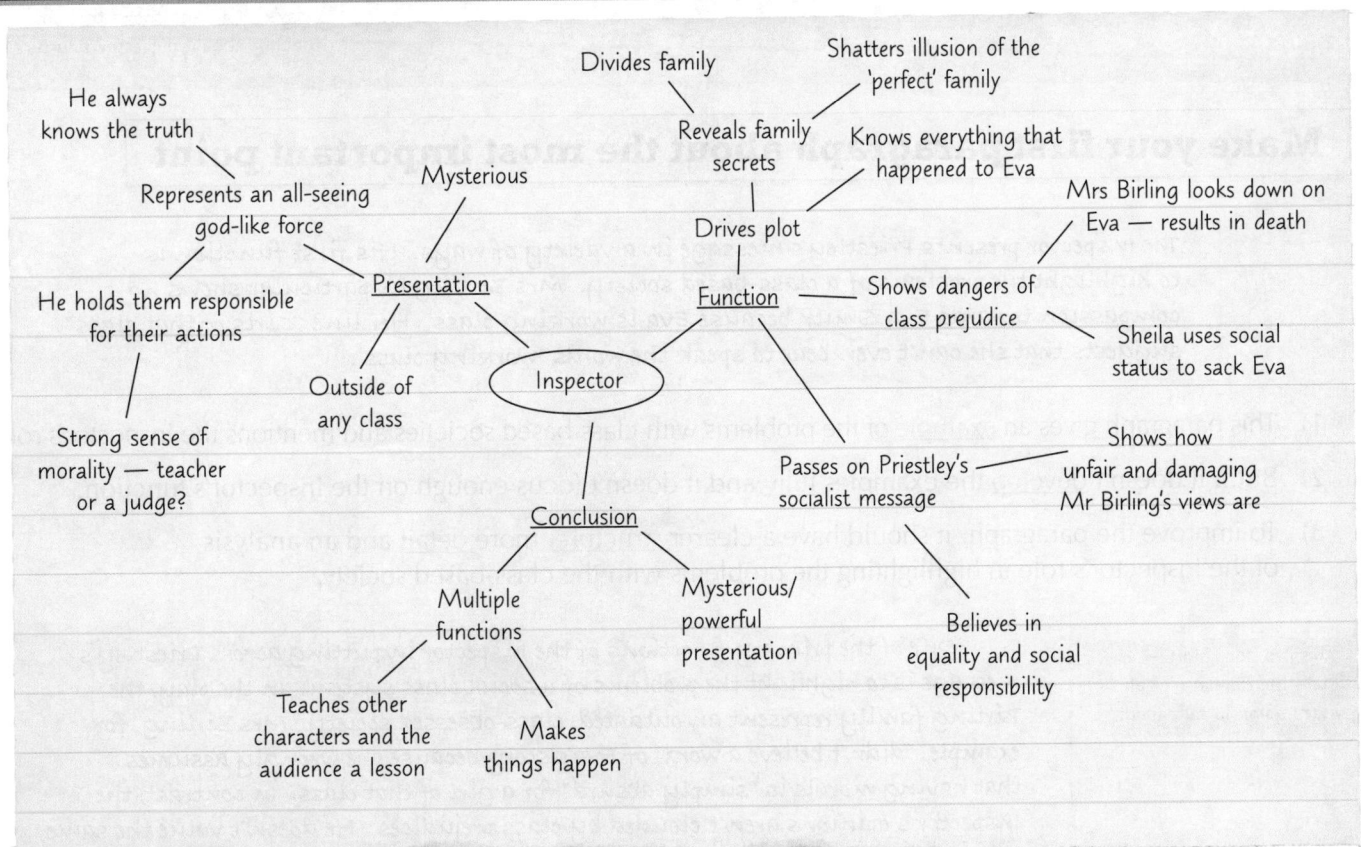

He always knows the truth

Represents an all-seeing god-like force

He holds them responsible for their actions

Strong sense of morality — teacher or a judge?

Mysterious

Presentation

Outside of any class

Inspector

Divides family

Reveals family secrets

Shatters illusion of the 'perfect' family

Knows everything that happened to Eva

Drives plot

Function

Shows dangers of class prejudice

Mrs Birling looks down on Eva — results in death

Sheila uses social status to sack Eva

Passes on Priestley's socialist message

Shows how unfair and damaging Mr Birling's views are

Conclusion

Multiple functions

Mysterious/ powerful presentation

Believes in equality and social responsibility

Teaches other characters and the audience a lesson

Makes things happen

What do examiners eat — eggs-ham-wiches of course...

The most important thing to remember is DON'T PANIC. Take a deep breath, read the questions, pick a good 'un, write a plan... take another deep breath and start writing. Leave 5 minutes at the end to check your answer too.

Worked Answer

These pages will show you how to turn an okay answer into a really good one that will impress the examiner.

Use your introduction to get off to a good start

These pages are all about how to word your sentences to impress the examiner, so we haven't included everything from the plan on page 59.

You might start with something like...

> Priestley's play is intended to make everyone aware of their social responsibility. The Inspector's main function is to clearly present this message.

1) This intro is okay. It mentions the message of social responsibility and the Inspector's main function.

2) It's also a good idea to use the key words in the question (like function) to give your essay focus and show the examiner you're on track and that you're thinking about the question from the start.

3) But there's still room for improvement...

This intro explains the author's message and the point of the play.

> In An Inspector Calls, Priestley wants to put across an important message of equality. Everyone needs to be aware of their responsibility to others, and that they should treat everyone fairly. The Inspector's main function is to present this message to the audience clearly and powerfully. In order to do this, Priestley presents the Inspector as a mysterious god-like character, so that his views seem to hold more weight.

This tells the examiner what the essay's about and shows that you've thought about your essay structure.

Make your first paragraph about the most important point

> The Inspector presents Priestley's message in a variety of ways. His first function is to highlight the problems of a class-based society. Mrs Birling in particular shows no compassion towards Eva Smith because Eva is working class. Her line "Girls of that class" suggests that she can't even bear to speak the words 'working class'.

1) This paragraph gives an example of the problems with class-based societies and mentions the Inspector's role.

2) But... it doesn't develop the examples fully and it doesn't focus enough on the Inspector's function.

3) To improve the paragraph, it should have a clearer structure, more detail and an analysis of the Inspector's role in highlighting the problems with the class-based society.

This is a good start — it tells the examiner what you're going to talk about.

> One of the primary functions of the Inspector in putting across Priestley's message is to highlight the problems of a social class system. In the play, the Birling family represent an outdated, class-obsessed society. Mrs Birling, for example, "didn't believe a word" of Eva's story because she wrongly assumes that having morals is "simply absurd" for a girl of that class. In contrast, the Inspector's opinions aren't clouded by class prejudices. He doesn't value the same things as the Birlings, for example, he's "never wanted to play" golf. He is classless, and so he sees things more clearly. This means the audience trusts his unbiased view of the situation — he functions as a god-like figure of moral judgement.

This is good because it includes a detailed example and it analyses and develops the point further.

Make sure you keep referring back to the question — one of the Inspector's functions is to judge and criticise the Birlings' prejudices.

Section Five — Exam Advice

Worked Answer

You need to make a variety of points

After you've talked about highlighting social problems you might start your next point like this:

> Priestley presents the Inspector as rude and confrontational in order to create tension in the play. This means he often clashes with the other characters.

1) It introduces the way that Priestley presents the Inspector in more detail.

2) You can make this paragraph better by giving more detailed examples and backing up points with quotes.

> Explaining how other characters view the Inspector is a good way of discussing his function.

> Priestley uses the reactions of the other characters to show that the Inspector's behaviour is unexpectedly blunt and aggressive. Mr Birling accuses him of being "offensive" and tries to "protest". But it's because he says things that a normal Inspector wouldn't dare to that the Inspector has power over them. For example, the Inspector's blunt anger makes Mrs Birling feel "cowed" and forces her to admit that she was "prejudiced against" Eva.

> Make sure you use a range of quotes, but don't quote huge chunks. Keep them snappy and relevant.

3) You could develop this further by describing how the Inspector also drives the plot forward:

> Using the word 'function' shows clearly that the answer relates to the question.

> The Inspector also has an important function in driving the plot forward, revealing how all the characters contributed to Eva's death. He appears to know everything, because of a "rough sort of diary" that Eva kept. But more importantly, he is in complete control of how information is revealed to the audience. Each character "must wait his turn" and when the Birlings get distracted by their own problems he interrupts "with authority" and forces the dialogue back to the developing story of Eva.

Finish your essay in style

You could say:

> In conclusion, the Inspector has many functions, but the main one is to put across Priestley's message of social responsibility. The Inspector is a powerful character because Priestley wants to strengthen his own message through the Inspector.

1) This conclusion's okay but it doesn't summarise how presentation helps develop the Inspector's function.

2) So to make it really impressive you could say something like...

> In conclusion, Priestley uses the Inspector for a variety of functions, and his presentation is shaped for these purposes. By making him classless he stands outside the Birlings' world and can make judgements on the characters along with the audience. He also drives the plot, forcing out the confessions which move the play to its conclusion, namely that "We are responsible for each other." He is not just another character; Priestley presents him as omniscient and god-like to aid his function as a judge and a teacher as well as the author's mouthpiece.

> This summarises some of the reasons Priestley has presented the character in such an unusual way.

> Make your last sentence really stand out — it's your last opportunity to impress the examiner.

Why do alligators write good essays? Their quotes are so snappy...

It seems like there's a lot to remember, but it's really quite simple. Just write a good intro and conclusion, make a range of points (one per paragraph) and put your most important point in paragraph one. Easy.

Index

The Characters from 'An Inspector Calls'

Phew! You should be an expert on *An Inspector Calls* by now. But if you want a bit of light relief and a quick recap of the play's plot, sit yourself down and read through *An Inspector Calls — The Cartoon...*

Arthur Birling

The Inspector

Sybil Birling

Gerald Croft

Eva Smith / Daisy Renton

Edna

Sheila Birling

Eric Birling

J. B. Priestley's 'An Inspector Calls'